THE SPIRITUAL NATURE OF REALITY

The Spiritual Nature of Reality

Christian Science Transforming the Universe

by

RICHARD CLAUDE HAW

The Bookmark
Santa Clarita, California

Haw, Richard C. (Richard Claude)
The spiritual nature of reality: Christian Science transforming the universe / by Richard Claude Haw. -- 1 st ed.
p. cm.
LCCN 2001098097
ISBN 0-930227-40-9

1. Christian Science. 2. Religion and science. 3. Philosophy and science. 4. Spiritual healing. 5. Prayer. I. Title.

BX6943.H39 2002 289.5
QBI33-276

Published by
The Bookmark
Post Office Box 801143
Santa Clarita, California 91380

INTRODUCTION

The early period in the Christian Science movement was concerned mainly with spiritual healing as this new religion spread throughout the world. But as the past century drew to a close, the depth and scope of Christian Science as a scientific discovery became increasingly evident. As the physics of the twentieth century progressed, physicists learned that there was more to the universe than material cause and effect. They began to verify Mrs. Eddy's statement that there is no matter. The medical world began to see the relationship between the mind and physical illness. Statements by prominent names in the scientific and medical worlds revealed how close both were coming to the fundamental ideas found in Christian Science.

Because of his background in both the sciences and Christian Science, Mr. Haw could see how the sciences are gradually developing rudimentary ideas found in Christian Science. He lived in Natal, South Africa. He was educated at the University of Natal, and through private study with the University of South Africa. He had a varied career as research chemist, topographical surveyor, farmer, conservation and agricultural officer, teacher, headmaster, and public relations and media executive. He was a deeply dedicated Christian Scientist.

Mr. Haw's background and interest in the natural sciences, coupled with his consecrated study of Christian Science, enabled him to foresee how this Science would eventually be recognized as a scientific discovery, accurately defining the realm of Mind that underlies all things. The first part of this book focuses on statements by well-known physicists as to the mental nature of atoms and the universe. Mr. Haw quotes them to show how the discoveries in physics are proving Mrs. Eddy's statement that "all is infinite Mind and its infinite manifestation." He then shows how the recognition that the human mind is the cause of all illness is moving doctors and psychologists towards the use of prayer as a healing power. This vision underlies most of his writings, including his book, *Mindpower and the Spiritual Dimension*.

Mr. Haw's writings are among the first to promote Christian Science as a scientific discovery. This Science is far more than a religion that heals through prayer alone. It is destined to transform world thought as humanity continues to recognize the mental nature of man and the universe. It is inevitable that the mental concept will gradually evolve into the spiritual concept as we learn more about the Mind hidden in the unseen realm. Thus in time science and religion will become one and the same, and be known as Christian Science.

The Spiritual Nature of Reality was written as an association address to be given to experienced Christian Scientists. Because his audience was familiar with the spiritual realm, Mr. Haw is especially forthright in the address when he relates the sciences to Christian Science. The healing experiences given towards the end of the book show Mr. Haw to be an outstanding Scientist who lived and demonstrated Christian Science in every way.

THE SPIRITUAL NATURE OF REALITY
Christian Science Transforming the Universe

by

Richard Claude Haw

This discussion is meant to indicate the unfolding of spiritual reality through absolute Christian Science. Spiritual reality unfolds as we advance in this understanding of the absolute allness and omnipotence of God, Spirit, good. Though these unfoldments may appear as changes in the outward scene, they are not really external to consciousness. They are simply clearer views of God's already existing, perfect spiritual creation appearing through the dissolving mist of materialism.

Christian Science is the only truly monistic or absolute system. It sticks unequivocally to its basic premise of one infinite God, Spirit, good. All other systems and religions are dualistic, and therefore, lack the spiritual dynamism which transforms that which appears as the outward scene. We work, not up to perfection, but out from the absolute standpoint.

The conceptual revolution that we are witnessing in the world today is undoubtedly due to this revolutionary spiritual idea which is leavening science, theology, and medicine. We are living in the most exciting age in all history. We are witnessing the unfoldment of the biblical prophecies regarding the End Times.

Divine Science, at work in human thought over the past century, has been loosening the rigid thought-patterns that constitute the phenomena of materialism. It is uncovering mortal illusions, exposing evil as a negation, and unfolding the realities of spiritual existence.

This advancing spiritual idea cannot be reversed any more than the sunrise can be checked since the ideas of Mind embody the full power of their divine Principle. The well-known writer, Lyall Watson, said in his book, *Lifetide*, "If an idea is planted, even if it be contrary to all existing evidence, it tends to grow, and sooner or later produces its own confirmation." It has also been said that there's nothing more powerful than an idea whose time has come.

The signs are unmistakable today that materialism is on the way out. This overturning of materialistic thought has generated the conflict described by Jesus in Matthew, chapter 24, portending the Second Coming of Christ, the Comforter, or divine Science. The chemicalization we see is due to the resistance of materialism to the spiritual idea which destroys it. The Discoverer and Founder of Christian Science, Mary Baker Eddy said, "The broadcast powers of evil, so conspicuous today, show themselves in the materialism and sensualism of the age, struggling against the advancing spiritual era." It is to be noted that it is materialism that is doing the struggling. St. Paul said we should "not be shaken in mind, nor troubled at the signs," for there shall come "a falling away first" before the "day of Christ" appears.

Mrs. Eddy states in *The People's Idea of God*, "Every step of progress is a step more spiritual. The great element of reform is not born of human wisdom; it draws not its life from human organizations; rather it is the crumbling away of material elements from reason, the translation of law back to its original language, — Mind, and the final unity between man and God."

The Conceptual Revolution

The world is on the threshold of a dramatic spiritual breakthrough with unprecedented implications for mankind. In referring to *Science and Health with Key to the Scriptures,* Mrs. Eddy said, "The textbook of Christian Science is transforming the universe." We shall be discussing some of the evidences of this transformation being brought about through the unfolding spiritual idea.

What is really happening is that Christian Science is translating what appears as matter into its original spiritual language. Mrs. Eddy states, "Science, understood, translates matter into Mind, rejects all other theories of causation, restores the spiritual and original meaning of the Scriptures, and explains the teachings and life of our Lord." She also states: "Matter is a misstatement of Mind." This shows there is only one reality — Mind's spiritual creation, which ignorant mortal mind misperceives as material. We are not, therefore, in the business of changing or destroying matter as such, but of re-translating so-called material phenomena back into spiritual terms.

Matter, as objective stuff, doesn't exist. It is a subjective misperception of spiritual reality, and we note that Mrs. Eddy says, "Every object in material thought will be destroyed." The true monism of divine Science declares there is only one reality — God, Spirit, Mind, and His infinite spiritual expression. In order to forward the spiritual revolution initiated by Christian Science, we need to grow beyond the dualistic sense that there is matter to be destroyed, disease to be healed, or evil to be overcome. Monism sees matter, evil or disease as inversions of reality to be re-translated. The so-called material universe is actually the divine universe misperceived. Our work is to translate "man and the universe back into Spirit," as our Leader states. "In proportion as this is done, man and the universe will be found harmonious and eternal."

Mrs. Eddy clearly tells us that what the human mind calls matter and spirit depends on the state of the perceiving consciousness. In *Science and Health*, writing of St. John's inspired vision in Revelation, she says, "This testimony of Holy Writ sustains the fact in Science, that the heavens and earth to one human consciousness, that consciousness which God bestows, are spiritual, while to another, the unillumined human mind, the vision is material. This shows unmistakably that what the human mind calls matter and spirit indicates states and stages of consciousness." We have the same scene, but two views of it. However solid matter may appear to the human senses, it is only a formation of thought, a subjective construct by those senses which are wrongly viewing some spiritual reality at hand.

The New Physics

One of the most exciting developments in the scientific world today is the way the new physics is approaching the standpoints of Christian Science regarding the mind/matter relationship. Classical physics' notions of an objectively material reality are rapidly giving way to quantum physics which sees all phenomena in terms of conscious apperception. Physics has now resolved matter into purely metaphysical terms. It regards consciousness as a primary reality — consciousness not merely interpreting but as actually forming the images we call physical phenomena.

Physicist John A. Wheeler says quantum mechanics "demolishes the view that the universe sits 'out there'" (*Genesis and Observership*), and Nobel physicist Eugene Wigner says quantum mechanics has "restored to physics the recognition of mind as a primary reality." (*Symmetrics and Reflections: Scientific Essays of Eugene P. Wigner*)

Dr. Wernher von Braun, NASA space scientist, recognized that the things we see as material are made up of mental concepts or thought-forms. Sir James Jeans, the British physicist/philosopher, said: "When we perceive an object, we perceive at most a few of its qualities." He said the so-called electric and magnetic forces "are not realities, . . . they are not even objective; but are subjective constructs which we have made for ourselves in our efforts to interpret nature." He continued: "The stream of knowledge is heading towards a non-mechanical reality; the universe begins to look more like a great thought than a great machine. . . The old dualism of mind and matter is disappearing, and matter is resolving into a creation or manifestation of mind." (*Physics and Philosophy*)

Cambridge University ethologist, W. H. Thorpe, says: "If we try to understand the human mind and its freedom of will, we find the universe dissolving into an infinity of mind which is, can only be, the sole way of understanding the universe." (*Purpose in a World of Chance*)

Dr. Allen D. Allen, of Algorithms Incorporated, says it is now an established theory that "the world is constructed from principles rather than from units of matter." He said, "We have decided that matter doesn't exist." Dr. Warren Weaver, one time Chairman of the Board of the American Association for the Advancement of Science, called matter an illusion. He said, "A table viewed with the precise tools of the atomic physicist, is a shadowy swirling set of electric charges, these charges themselves being vague and elusive. So viewed, the table loses its large-scale illusion of solidity. . . When the scientist forces his thinking down to basic levels, a wholly new and strangely abstract set of ideas comes into play. Solids are not really solid. 'Real objects' are not even composed, as physicists thought half a century ago, of sub-microscopic atoms like billiard balls. . . . The scientist knows that the everyday reality of the table or rock is an illusion, and that reality is in fact a very subtle, evasive, and somewhat abstract business." (*Look Magazine,* April 5,1955) Scientists tell us that these whirling electrical forces that matter is made of are comprised of subatomic particles which aren't really material at all. They are virtually all empty space. In fact, if all the empty spaces in the atoms comprising an adult human body could be squeezed out, all we'd be left with would be a minute speck that could be put on the point of a pin!

What, then, is this speck made of? Nobel physicist Wernher Heisenberg says, "The smallest units of matter are not in fact physical objects in the ordinary sense; they are forms, ideas, which can only be described unambiguously in mathematical terms." (*Frontiers of Modern Scientific Philosophy and Humanism*)

Well, if matter is simply made up of ideas, or mathematical forms, (and mathematics is purely metaphysical), what do we make of the shape, size and solidity that material objects appear to have? Another Nobel physicist, Erwin Schrodinger, tells us that shape doesn't have to have matter to form it. He says, "The habit of everyday language deceives us, and seems to require, whenever we hear the word 'shape' or 'form' pronounced, that it must be the shape of *something,* that a material substratum is required to take on a shape. But when you come to the ultimate particles constituting matter, there seems to be no point in thinking of them again as consisting of something material. They are, as it were, *pure shape,* nothing but shape; what turns up again and again in successive observations is this shape, not an individual speck of material." (*Science & Humanism: Physics in Our Time*)

In their efforts to interpret reality, physicists are inevitably being driven into the realm of metaphysics, since matter has now become recognized as a mental phenomenon. Einstein said anyone studying physics long enough is inevitably led into metaphysics. (This was mentioned after a Wednesday evening Testimony Meeting at a church in New York, as related by George Nay, when Einstein referred to Christian Science as "a wonderful thing.")

Such enlightened views of matter's insubstantiality are leading to new conceptions of fundamental reality. Materialism is now obsolete. The well-known scientist, J. S. Haldane, wrote: "Materialism, once a scientific theory, is now the fatalistic creed of thousands, but materialism is nothing better than superstition on the same level as belief in witches and devils." (*The Sciences and Philosophy*) Dr. A. Taylor, a Fellow of the American Association for the Advancement of Science, said: "Physics is necessarily becoming more metaphysical as its research progresses. . . . The materialistic hypothesis certainly does not add to the objectivity of scientific research, but rather brings to it a quality more weird than a tale from the Arabian Nights." (*Consciousness and Reality,* edited by Muses and Young)

The materialistic mind-set that sustained the classical physics' notions of objective reality is rapidly being transmuted, and great conceptual changes are occurring on the frontiers of thought. This must surely be the result of the unfolding spiritual idea promoted by Christian Science over the past century.

The physicists have taken their first step in metaphysics, by resolving "things into thoughts." They are seeing things in terms of the *materially* mental, as concepts of the human mind. They are on the threshold of the next and ultimate step in metaphysics, that of "exchanging the objects of sense for the ideas of Soul" — of seeing reality in terms of the *divine* Mind's spiritually mental ideas.

Basil Hiley of Birkbeck College, London, believes that physicists have now been brought to the point where they have to consider the possibility of "radically new views of reality" (*New Scientist,* Jan. 6, '83) This is because physicists have been trying to explain the universe on the impossible basis of material sense instead of spiritual sense. Mrs. Eddy says it will remain an enigma so long as it is so regarded. There has to be a transcendence above the first level of metaphysics which merely mentalizes matter and resolves things into thoughts. It is only by exchanging the objects of sense for the ideas of Soul that we come to the understanding of divine reality.

Dr. Sydney Drell of Stanford University says physicists are today advancing closer to the description of reality given in the Bible and are "in search of a sort of Holy Grail, with a faith that there is some elegant, single, beautiful system in nature to be discovered." (*Daedalus 1977*)

Dr. A. Taylor (ibid) says, "Scientific knowledge has revealed a universe of meaning, plan, ideation, intelligence. The more that scientists are able to translate the book of nature, the more astounding the wisdom revealed. We are confident that the previous emphasis on materialism will soon be discarded." (*Consciousness and Reality,* edited by Muses and Young)

Physicist/philosopher Sir Arthur Eddington came near to seeing monistic spiritual reality when he wrote: "When science has progressed the furthest, the mind has but regained from nature what the mind has put into nature. . . . The nature of all reality is spiritual, not material, not a dualism of matter and spirit." (*Arthur Stanley Eddington,* by Douglas)

The scientific world is now ripe for what Christian Science has to say concerning the nature of reality. Mrs. Eddy provides deep insights for physicists to ponder, such as the following in *Science and Health:* "From the infinite elements of the one Mind emanate all form, color, quality and quantity, and these are mental, both primarily and secondarily." And, "The divine Mind maintains all identities from a blade of grass to a star, as distinct and eternal." "Spirit is the life, substance, and continuity of all things. We tread on forces. Human knowledge calls them forces of matter, but divine Science declares that they belong wholly to divine Mind, are inherent in this Mind, and so restores them to their rightful home and classification." Also, "The compounded minerals and aggregated substances composing the earth, the relations which constituent masses hold to each other, the magnitudes, distances, and revolutions of the celestial bodies, are of no real importance, when we remember that they all must give place to the spiritual fact by the translation of man and the universe back into Spirit. In proportion as this is done, man and the universe will be found harmonious and eternal." Such statements show that Christian Science holds the solutions to the quantum paradoxes and has explanations for all phenomena.

The spiritual ideas constituting reality are the archetypes of which the humanly perceived phenomena are symbolical forms.

These forms are constructed by the human mind from the now obsolete basis of materiality. The pictured image seen as a tree, for instance, is a mental model, and its apparent qualities of color, shape, size, texture and solidity are the brain's symbolical interpretations.

The brain does not really create anything, nor does it really think in the creative teleological sense. It is a computer-like entity that receives mental impressions, classifies them, and stores them for use in coping with the problems of human experience. The brain spins its own patterns, which are pictured images of its own concepts of reality, but these illusory images are based upon its educated presuppositions of a material reality. Now the physicists have demolished this supposed material reality as an illusion.

Here it is well to define *illusion.* We usually think of an illusion as referring to something that doesn't really exist, but a dictionary defines it as "a false sense-impression of something actually present." (Chambers) There are no vacuums in Mind. There is something there, but it has been misconstrued by the human mind.

Monism and Dualism

I think this is important to understand in our metaphysical practice because one sometimes hears it said by Christian Scientists that "there's nothing there" when dealing with some problem. There is something there, some idea of divine Mind, and the illusion called a problem needs to be seen in its true aspect. We are also sometimes inclined to speak of reality behind some phenomenon. This is dualistic, appropriate perhaps in the early stages of one's understanding, but we must rise to the monistic understanding of absolute Science which accepts only one reality, the divine and spiritual. In this monistic understanding, the symbol, illusion, or counterfeit disappears in the light of spiritual reality. There is not one class of phenomena to be changed or destroyed so that divine reality can appear. The reality is already there, instead, and divine metaphysics reveals it as the *sole* reality.

Our Leader tells us, "Every material belief hints the existence of spiritual reality; and if mortals are instructed in spiritual things, it will be seen that material belief, in all its manifestations, reversed, will be found the type and representative of verities priceless, eternal, and just at hand." (*Miscellaneous Writings*)

To attempt to destroy something implies that there is some entity to be destroyed, and this is dualistic. We do not really destroy or deny anything but false beliefs, although in absolute Science there aren't any false beliefs because divine Mind is All. True monism works only from the basis of God's absolute allness. Geoffrey Barratt wrote in the Spanish *Christian Science Herald* of November 1977: "The only side to work on is total Spirit and total spirituality. Otherwise, we're not working metaphysically, but laboring mortally."

The spiritual facts are the sole realities of being. Whatever would appear to deny this is an inverted view by a suppositional mind which is ignorant of divine reality. This monistic understanding of reality is the unique contribution of Christian Science to advancing thought. This is what is pressing the questing thought of mankind through the finite parameters of materialism. The prayers and thoughts of millions of Christian Scientists over the decades have been dissolving rigid mental barriers and limitations, and freeing thought to accept and explore the boundless realm of Mind. The astounding technological advances of our age may *appear* as material changes, but they are actually higher unfoldments of reality — transmutations of the *mental* patternings called matter. (Physicists now see matter in terms of patterns of energy, a wave of forces subtended by consciousness.)

Quantum physics is being driven irresistibly towards the standpoints of Christian Science regarding the nature of matter. All the standpoints embodied in the first sentence of "the scientific statement of being" in our textbook would now be corroborated by the world's top natural scientists. Once totally opposed by the mainstream of human thinking, this "scientific statement of being" is now in the vanguard of advancing thought.

No physicist or biologist or psychologist has ever seen mind or intelligence *in* matter. But they have seen matter exhibiting the *effects* of mind or intelligence. None have ever found any real nexus between life and matter, but they have seen matter exhibiting the effects of a life-force. Certainly, the physicists now would acknowledge there is no substance in matter, and have said as much. As for there being any truth in matter, physicists call matter an illusion, and no illusion can be truth. People *claim* they can see life, substance, intelligence and power in matter, but all they have seen is so-called matter exhibiting the *effects* of life, intelligence and power.

Physics Obsolete?

Physicists and astrophysicists are nonplussed about the implications of "black holes" or collapsed stars in outer space, because they portend the collapse of all the laws of physics. An enormous star, millions of times the size of our earth, may collapse into nothing. Astrophysicist Jonathan Grindley says this is a "very disturbing idea." (*Time Magazine,* Sept. *4, 1978)* And physicist John A. Wheeler says the implications threaten "the framework for everything one ever called a law of physics." (*Genesis and Observership,* and *Time Magazine,* Sept. *4, 1978*)

Although this is disturbing to physicists, it isn't disturbing to Christian Scientists because the implications point to the basic truth of what Mrs. Eddy wrote concerning matter and the nature of reality. She said in *Science and Health,* "Material substances or mundane formations, astronomical calculations, and all the paraphernalia of speculative theories, based on the hypothesis of material law, or life and intelligence resident in matter, will ultimately vanish, swallowed up in the infinite calculus of Spirit."

The present stage the world is experiencing is a necessary prelude to the advanced understanding which Christian Science reveals of the totally spiritual nature of all reality. The mental nature of things is becoming widely understood, and as the NASA Director of Astrophysics, Charles Pellerin Jr., says, "A lot of people are thinking that the time may be right for an overthrow of physical law." (*The Christian Science Monitor,* Sept. 22, 1984)

Christian Science is bringing the realization that everything that exists is the expression of Mind, Spirit, God. The millennium awaits this recognition. It is already here. Mrs. Eddy says, "The substance, Life, intelligence, Truth and Love, which constitute Deity, are reflected by His creation; and when we subordinate the false testimony of the corporeal senses to the facts of Science, we shall see this true likeness and reflection everywhere." (*Science and Health*)

Christ Jesus' statement that the kingdom of heaven is at hand, within us, as a state of consciousness, shows that all the things of nature — the trees, rocks, mountains — are spiritual formations forever held in perfection by the divine Mind that created them.

All the phenomena of existence — our bodies, businesses, homes, and experiences — are really spiritual expressions of God. When we learn to see the things of technological civilization as in fact perfect expressions of divine Mind, we will find them conforming to the laws of divine Principle. The economy is the ceaseless activity of Love, blessing all mankind. Living, moving, and having our being in God, in the midst of the kingdom of heaven, we possess all good — in fact, we are the good that God is expressing.

Physicist David Bohm approaches the monistic understanding of reality when he speaks of a "single totality of being" embracing all phenomena in a "higher-dimensional reality." This may be the physicist's way of describing the oneness and all-inclusiveness of God, universal Mind.

Stirrings in the Medical World

The exciting developments in the world of physics are also affecting other branches of science, including medicine. Though the medical world is fighting a rear guard action against Christian Science which challenges its claims to be the only legitimate healing system, it is steadily being undermined by the unfolding spiritual idea, as we shall see.

But, in the meantime, Modern Medicine is aggressively promoting its brand of materialism. One has only to look at what's portrayed by today's pervasive communications media to see how television, cinema, magazines and newspapers are full of medical propaganda. They seldom fail to include scenes of accidents, diseases, ambulances, hospitals, doctors and nurses, with all the paraphernalia of medical technology, surgery and drugs. Descriptions of disease instill fear, and all have the effect of reinforcing material beliefs and promoting *materia medica* as the remedy for all the world's human ills.

This constitutes a pervasive mental force that is antagonistic to Christian Science, and we need to be alert to it. Mrs. Eddy says: "By universal consent, mortal belief has constituted itself a law to bind mortals to sin, sickness and death." (*Science* and *Health*) She also states: "The universal belief in physics weighs against the high and mighty truths of Christian metaphysics. This erroneous general belief, which sustains medicine and produces all medical results works against Christian Science; and the percentage of power on the side of this Science must mightily outweigh the power of popular belief in order to heal a single case of disease." (ibid)

This indicates the importance of nullifying these claims in our practice of Christian Science. Edward Kimball said that patients are sick according to a law of general belief, and that this false mesmeric law must be broken in order to free the patient.

The whole of mortal existence is a state of mesmerism, and medical beliefs are one of its most insidious claims, often coming in the guise of good, and there is no doubt that Modern Medicine does set out to do good according to its own lights. The great majority of nurses and doctors are motivated by love and compassion, and without their humanitarian ministrations, human suffering would be so much the greater.

But, having said this, medical practice is only a palliative, as many doctors would readily admit. Even its spectacular surgical achievements do nothing to heal the errant mentality that binds people to the syndrome of errors associated with materialism. The medical profession does not offer any transcendent remedy. They are trapped in the sophisticated mumbo jumbo of Modern Medicine that the public has been brainwashed into accepting.

Most doctors now well understand the placebo effect of drugs and the dangers attached to drugging, but continue to prescribe drugs because they know no alternative, and people have come to expect drugs as the panacea for all ills. Many books are meanwhile coming out which reveal the enormous damage caused by the drugging system. The United States Commissioner of Food and Drugs said, "We have created in America a culture of drugs. We have produced an environment in which people come naturally to expect they can take a pill for every problem, that we can find satisfaction and health and happiness in a handful of tablets or a few grains of powder." He said drug advertising designed to sell, motivates physicians to prescribe them and consumers to buy them. Advertisements also promote images of disease in order to sell the drugs supposed to cure them.

In the United States more than 700 million pills are consumed every day, and, despite the awful toll and side effects, the public continues to clamor for more. A book by Melville and Johnson called *Cured to Death,* says as many people die from side-effects of drugs as die in road accidents, and *that* figure annually exceeds those killed in the Vietnam war.

Some authorities say that one in every twenty hospital admissions is due to drugs and doctors' errors. Doctors' errors, in fact, constitute the fastest-growing cause of disease. So much so, that chairs of iatrogenic medicine are now established in many medical schools to study the problem. (Iatrogenic means diseases caused by doctors.)

Countless cases of drug-induced illness, malfunctioning, deformity, and death are on record, and a well-known professor of medicine in South Africa, Harry Grant-Whyte, has publicly described the abuse of drugs as "a greater threat to Western Civilization than the atom bomb." (Professor Grant-Whyte incidentally described my book, *Mindpower and the Spiritual Dimension,* as "an outstanding thesis, remarkable, informative, fascinating," and he recommends it to his audiences as "the book that has all the answers.")

The wrongness of the drug scene, boosting as it does the profits of the pharmaceutical industry, is highlighted by the proven fact that drugs have only the power that faith puts in them. Numerous experiments with placebos or dummy drugs carried out in medical and psychological laboratories have shown this to be true — a fact Mrs. Eddy discovered more than a century ago. Even the most virulent and lethal drugs have only the power that thought gives to them.

In the book, *A Century of Christian Science Healing,* a Christian Scientist who was a professor of chemistry had an experience that showed what would normally have been regarded as an instantly lethal contact with potassium cyanide crystals had no effect on him. And I myself can testify to two similar instances in my own experience involving cyanide and arsenic.

To sustain its credibility and power, Modern Medicine and the pharmaceutical industry are in cahoots and resort to expensive advertising and propaganda. Competing systems of healing are attacked. But the shortcomings of Modern Medicine are being exposed by many enlightened doctors. In his book, *Limits to*

Medicine: Medical Nemesis, Ivan Illich says: "The medical establishment has become a major threat to health, and a nightmarish spiritual and physical agent of destruction."

Dr. Robert Mendelsohn, in his book, *Confessions of a Medical Heretic,* cites a U.S. Congressional Sub-Committee's statement that "2.4 million operations in the United States annually are unnecessary. They cost $4 billion and kill 12,000 people annually. Of the 250,000 deaths following surgery annually, the study showed that half needed no surgery or medical treatment at all."

He says, "I believe that Modern Medicine's treatments for disease are seldom effective, and they are often more dangerous than the disease they are designed to treat. . . . The entire diagnostic procedure . . . is a seldom useful ritual. X-rays are especially dangerous and can lead to diabetes, stroke, cataracts, cardiovascular disease, and genetic problems in the case of pregnancies; 4,000 deaths are annually attributed directly to medical and dental radiation."

Dr. Mendelsohn continues: "A hospital is like a war. You should try your best to stay out of it. The X-ray machine is the most pervasive and most dangerous tool in the doctor's office." He says the Church of Modern Medicine is a "Church of Death."

Dr. Mendelsohn calls for action for people to liberate themselves completely from Modern Medicine, and he recommends what he calls the New Medicine. This looks at man from a more holistic and religious standpoint. Holistic therapy moves away from treating people as hunks of matter, and it is now a strongly growing movement.

Many doctors today are becoming disenchanted with Modern Medicine and turning to systems that treat people from a mental and religious viewpoint. They are seeing man more as an integrated, individual being, not just a collection of organs and limbs. They are treating people as embraced in an environment of love and completeness and wholeness, with the religious element being regarded as of prime importance.

One of these practitioners of the New Medicine is Dr. Irving Oyle who teaches at the University of California. He has written several books, including *The Healing Mind; Time, Space and Mind;* and *The New American Medicine Show.* Dr. Oyle takes up the findings of modern physics which show that matter isn't substance but a form of conscious perception. The physicists, he says, have reduced all the matter in a human body to something that isn't there at all, and Dr. Oyle, therefore, feels that he can no longer think of treating it in the traditional way. He says the findings of physics foreshadow the imminent downfall of the cult of scientific materialism on which the practice of medicine is based. He states that the U.S.A. spends about $200 billion a year on using an obsolete approach without significantly affecting mortality rates. He is fully persuaded that the mind is primary, and matter is simply the reflection of what is in consciousness, so the obvious remedy lies with improving consciousness.

The tragedy about all this is that the real remedy for every problem has been freely available for more than a century, and we Christian Scientists haven't done as well as we might to promote it and to heal according to its limitless potential. It is because of this spiritual void that there's been a tidalwave of drugs, both medicinal and psychogenic, sweeping over the world. The barrenness and meaninglessness of mortal existence drives people to drugs and alcohol for escape and is also the cause of disease. With the collapse of materialism, people are floundering in an existential maelstrom, being blown hither and thither by semi-metaphysical and material palliatives.

Time, Aging

Christian Science, of course, has the answers for all human problems, but it's quite apparent that we need to do much better than we have done in leading on the ages. And here it may be appropriate to deal with the question of time and its syndrome of errors, especially of aging. The belief that we live in a space-time world is part of the Adam dream that expresses itself in beliefs of aging and obsolescence. As an element of materialism, time constricts and limits at every turn, but, since matter, space and time are mortally mental concepts without actual reality, human birth, maturity, decay, death, and all forms of limitation are merely subjective errors of mortal mind.

Physicist Sir James Jeans said, "Time, like conceptual space, exists only in the mind of the thinker." He says the concept of space "has no existence of any kind except in the mind of man who is creating it by thinking it." (*Physics and Philosophy*) Time is obviously relative. Two weeks on vacation is not the same as two weeks on a diet! Einstein said space and time are creations of our own imagination. Neither could be measured without matter to measure or measure with, and we have already seen that the physicists themselves have demolished matter as a substantial reality.

It is these illusions of matter, space and time, which underlie the Adamic beliefs of human birth, maturity, disease, decay, death, as well as the obsolescence and destruction of useful things. These illusions are but subjective errors of mortal belief. Christian Science has come to show us the eternal facts of being which apply not only to our bodily existence, but to all the phenomena we see around us. Mortal belief says we are born into matter and die out of it, with a lot of trouble in between. It says things become old, wear out, and become obsolete; but inasmuch as the sole reality of existence is spiritual, perfect and eternal, the facts of spiritual existence should be translatable into harmonious human experience. The spiritual ideas which constitute reality were never born, and cannot become old, sick, wear out, or die.

Scientists tell us that time is a subjective concept, and that there is no such entity in the absolute. At the speed of light, time stops altogether, and if we were to go on a spaceship at that speed, we would never age though centuries may be recorded on earth. Scientists also tell us that an object traveling at a speed approaching that of light would begin to get smaller and would shrink to nothing at the speed of light.

I've already mentioned what physicists say about the atoms comprising a human body — that if all the empty spaces in the atoms could be squeezed out, all we'd be left with would be a minute speck, which Nobel physicist Heisenbers says isn't material at all but is comprised of ideas. Then where does birth, disease, decay, or death fit in such a picture? They are simply mortal mind's projected illusions based on its educated beliefs in a supposed material reality. They are therefore correctable through the spiritual truths taught in Christian Science. But, of course, this will require of us immense spiritual growth to demonstrate it.

Christ Jesus declared that his followers should "not see death." He also said, "This is life eternal;" and in St. Thomas' Gospel from the Dead Sea Scrolls, he said, "I am come to destroy the works of birth." Mrs. Eddy tells us that all our problems stem from the Adam dream, but we seem to defer consideration of the implications of her deeper meanings and of Jesus' statements.

Aging is a phenomenon of mortal mind, and the story from *The Lancet,* which Mrs. Eddy quotes in *Science and Health,* shows that decrepitude is an illusion and not a necessity of nature. Mrs. Eddy also has stated that it is possible to reverse the manifestations of aging through right thinking. The body is a mental concept and doesn't know how old it is. We tell *it* by recording ages, celebrating birthdays, and going along with prattle about age.

Dr. Irving Oyle, whom I quoted just now, says we program our brains with beliefs about growing old, and that this acts as a direct command to the body to do just that. Dr. Oyle says there is now a turnaround among enlightened doctors, and they are beginning to look at consciousness as the determinant of experience. They are beginning to realize there is no separation between mind and body, and that the body is a function of consciousness. Some doctors are now saying the body should go on for 150 years. (Amplified Bible — The seventy year life-span was a penalty imposed on the Israelites for their disobedience to God at Kadesh-Barnea. The curse was subsequently lifted.) Doctors are saying that aging is a mental phenomenon and is due to a "time neurosis, a morbid fear of the passage of time." This was said at a Medical Symposium in the United States. Another doctor at the symposium said, "Years alone have no effect in bringing about degenerative disorders. Every human tissue is endowed with potential immortality." He also said that degenerative disorders are associated with faulty elimination and the accumulation of poisons.

Dr. Frederick Swartz said at an American Academy of General Practice Convention in 1965: "The so-called infirmities of age . . . are not caused by the passage of time. Time is a measure, not a force. Aging, although it represents an accumulation of time units, is still a measure, not, a force."

Aging is an accumulation of mortal beliefs, and the Christian Science response to this is to show how to neutralize and eliminate poisonous grieving, resentful, hateful, sensual thinking through the purifying action of Christ, Truth, and expressing qualities of Love — purity and spirituality. Paul adjures us to "put off concerning the former conversation the old man, which is corrupt according to the deceitful lusts; and be renewed in the spirit of your mind; and that ye put on the new man, which after God is created in righteousness and true holiness."

It is important for us to handle the Adam dream, and the world beliefs of mortal history. They are universal mesmerisms. We live in the eternal *now* of God's infinite perfection. Man isn't an entity programmed for a mortal or temporal span, but he lives in eternity, free from beliefs of matter, space and time. Man was never born into matter, and, like the ray of the sun, he is ever being created brand new. He is forever untouched by mortal beliefs of birth, decay and death, and belief in genes conferring mortal characteristics.

We don't have to "pass on." Our aim must be ascension, not dying out of mortality. When someone appears to pass on, nothing has really happened to that individual. The mourners see the projection of their own mortal beliefs and proceed to bury *their* false concept of that individual. In *Science and Health* Mrs. Eddy says, "Mortals awake from the dream of death with bodies unseen by those who think that they bury the body." She said of Edward Kimball after he had passed on, that "he is here now as veritably as when he visited me a year ago. If we would awaken to this recognition, we should see him here, and realize that he never died; thus demonstrating the fundamental truth of Christian Science." (*Miscellany*) Mrs. Eddy's article entitled "Life" in the *Christian Science Sentinel* of February 2, 1918, is worth our study.

A contemporary of Mrs. Eddy's, Rev. J. Paterson-Smyth, (who contributed to *Dummelow's Bible Commentary)* wrote a book, *The Gospel of the Hereafter,* published in 1908. In it he states: "There is no death. . . . Human life is the most exciting, romantic adventure in the universe; it is going on stage after stage, and then on again through infinite eternities." He said, "I am the permanent being behind all I am, and remain the same because God is the same. God created you and lovingly planned for you your magnificent destiny. This life is but the first stage of God's life for you, the kindergarten or caterpillar stage. In 5000 years that spiritual being looking out from behind the mask of your face will be living still, feeling still, thinking still. That which you call death is but birth into a new and more exciting career, stretching away into the future. No wildest fairy tale could suggest the wonder of its possibilities as it passes into the new adventure of the life beyond."

Although Rev. Paterson-Smyth is dualistic in speaking of life as passing through stages, he does see the endlessness of life. In truth, the life we are living now is God, divine Life, being expressed as us. Ivimy Gwalter in her article, "The Coincidence of the Human and Divine," said, "The human is not an imperfect state of existence which will sometime become spiritual, but an imperfect sense of the divinity which is here and now the actual, the tangible, the true."

Man's only identity is the compound of divine and eternal qualities. These are just as substantial to spiritual sense as the human appears to the material senses. The human appearance seems pretty solid, but it is entirely mental, as the physicists now acknowledge. In the Transfiguration experience, Moses and Elias appeared with Jesus, and they were recognized by Peter, James and John.

The facts of eternal spiritual existence apply not only to our bodies, but, Mrs. Eddy says, "to all the phenomena of existence." (*Science and Health*) This naturally includes our churches, homes, cars, and even our appliances. The children of Israel's shoes and clothes "waxed not old" in their forty years in the wilderness. A friend of mine used to give her fridge a treatment when it gave trouble, and another "healed" a watch that was said to be useless.

We need to translate everything back into Spirit and see all as ideas of eternal Mind forever maintained in perfection by God. A mechanism is no less a compound of thought than our bodies, and we should begin to exercise the dominion God gave to man by bringing to bear on all aspects of experience the power of Mind over the temporal phenomena of materialism. All the things of existence reflect states and stages of consciousness, and through the advancing spiritual idea, Christian Science is unfolding the kingdom of heaven at hand.

We live in the eternal now of God's infinite perfection, and this divine fact is the law of correction to the Adam dream with all its delusions of a mortal history, past or present suffering, heredity, and fears of future error.

Because there is no time, there is no mortal history. It is but the record of dreams, and dreams have no reality. God always has been All-in-all, so there never was a mortal birth, inharmonious experience, or death. All there is to such dreams is our *present* perception of them, and this is correctable through the understanding of God's eternal nowness, allness and perfection. The past is the present reality misunderstood. Nothing is going on, or ever has gone on, but God expressing Himself, and that's perfect. Animal magnetism claims to hold us in belief of a space-time world with inharmonious experiences. These may rankle and produce disease, but this serpentine belief cannot be true since God is All-in-all.

Christian Science brings a new light to the subject of prophecy. The common belief that prophecy is the foretelling of future events that must be awaited before they can be fulfilled is a fatalistic and pagan outlook. Whatever is true in the future is true *now.* What is needed is enlightenment, not time. When the biblical prophets foretold evil, it was only that they saw this unfolding as a result of the people's ungodlike thinking and living. Good is ever-present, and evil is never present. The prophets spoke in the grammatical form known as the "prophetic perfect." Their "prophecies" were of good as a *now* thing. It was the Bible's scribes who put it into the future tense because they thought the people wouldn't understand since evil seemed so apparent all around them.

The Adam dream is the serpent's biggest lie. Mrs. Eddy says it is "the foundation of mortal discord." It must be nullified in our treatments. Man's preexistence and coexistence with eternal Life, God, is established fact and is law to the Adam-dream and its syndrome of errors.

Handling Animal Magnetism

What is holding our movement back is unhandled animal magnetism. As in Mrs. Eddy's time, there seems to be a reluctance to come to grips with this sum total of evil. Among those who neglect this duty which our Leader demanded we discharge daily,

(See *Church Manual,* Art. VIII, Sect. 6) are some who fear to uncover the iniquity of evil and others who think that because evil is really nothing, we needn't bother to handle the claim. Both are fatal errors, for Mrs. Eddy makes it perfectly clear that animal magnetism's effects on those who do not resist it "lead to moral and to physical death," as she states in *Science and Health.* "The dangerous error to students is not seeing error, insensibility to the presence of error," Mrs. Eddy said.

In her article, "Ways That Are Vain" in *Miscellany,* Mrs. Eddy says: "The intricate method of animal magnetism is the essence, the spirit of evil that makes mankind drunken," and she castigates those who are "too cowardly, too ignorant, or too wicked to uncover [it]." In *Science and Health,* Mrs. Eddy writes: "Many are willing to open the eyes of the people to the power of good resident in divine Mind, but they are not so willing to point out the evil in human thought and expose evil's hidden mental ways of accomplishing iniquity." In the next paragraph she brings out the necessity for exposing it, and asks: "Who is telling mankind of the foe in ambush?" Mrs. Eddy said of one worker who wasn't coming to grips with animal magnetism, "Your head is way above in the stars while the enemy is filling your body with bullets."

Our Leader also italicizes the words "mental assassins" in her writings obviously for a reason, and she herself never let up in handling the serpent. In *Science and Health* she tells us, "A knowledge of error and its operations must precede that understanding of Truth which destroys error." Unless we know what the serpent is up to, we are not likely to be roused to do our work about it.

In *Miscellaneous Writings* Mrs. Eddy makes this rousing call to arms: "The great battle of Armageddon is upon us. The powers of evil are leagued together in secret conspiracy against the Lord and His Christ, as expressed and operative in Christian Science. Large numbers, in desperate malice, are engaged day and night in organizing action against us. Their feeling and purpose are deadly, and they have sworn enmity against our standard-bearers."

This is no mealy-mouthed statement, but an imperative call to us which I believe is largely unheeded in our movement today. Our Leader calls for our enlistment in this "greatest and holiest of all causes," and this demands of us the proper handling of the claims of evil. In a letter to Adam Dickey, Mrs. Eddy said the survival of the Cause of Christian Science rests upon our handling animal magnetism.

We cannot afford to be naive about the serpent's *claims.* Due to the great mental chemicalization going on today, animal magnetism is more virulent, subtle and widespread than ever before. The mental atmosphere is flooded with thoughts of evil, crime, violence, immorality, hate, disease, disaster, death and the spirit of antichrist. This, coupled with the purposeful deployment of mental powers as in hypnotism, voodoo, witchcraft, psychic forces, telepathy, and telekineses, has ballooned the serpent into the "Great Red Dragon, swollen with sin and ripe for destruction." It is the mentalizing of matter that is making this period so fraught with danger. It stands to reason that if matter becomes seen as a subjective mental phenomenon, then thought can do things to it and with it. Mrs. Eddy tells us that matter is the "substratum of mortal mind," and that "things are thoughts." It follows that whatever mortal mind thinks, this is liable to be manifested. So long as matter was regarded as objective stuff, independent of the mind, it wasn't as easy for mortal mind to work iniquity. Matter is simply a solidified form of mortal thought, so it is really no mystery that thought can change matter's forms or move it about.

This is the most dangerous age in history, when matter is becoming widely known as a phenomenon of the human mind. In the textbook, Mrs. Eddy says: "Mortal mind sees what it believes, as certainly as it believes what it sees. It feels, hears, and sees its own thoughts." Here we have the explanation for psychic and paranormal phenomena, witchcraft, hypnotism, and so on. Our experience is governed by our beliefs. A first grader had an explanation for the fire at his school. He said, "I knew it would happen because we have been practising for it all year." Christian Science exposes all evil or error as a mesmeric picturing of mortal thought. Matter is comprised of projected mental patternings. These mental patternings, however, remain in the realm of belief, and Christian Science shows their illusory nature. They are insubstantial shadows of the realities within the divine Mind.

The well-known science writer, Lyall Watson, says in his book, *Lifetide,* that human consciousness is "a state of grand illusion," but he also warns in his book, *Supernature,* of the dangers of evil thinking. He states: "There is no doubt that someone who believes that he has been bewitched can think himself into illness or even death." Dr. Watson then refers to new research into mental powers, which he says "make it plain that you don't necessarily have to think your own destructive thoughts. Someone else can think them up and point them at you."

Australian aborigines have a ceremony in which bones are pointed at the mental image of someone in disfavour, and this has been known to produce death, even where the individual is unaware of the pointing. Many deaths are on record from African witchcraft, which is but another form of hypnotism. People can be hypnotized to experience or do almost anything, a fact confirmed by an internationally known hypnotist, Peter Casson.

In Denmark in 1954, a man was jailed for life for hypnotizing someone to commit armed robbery and murder. People can be hypnotized at a distance and without their knowledge, and suggestions can be made to take effect even months or years later. Now, all these things happen in the realm of belief, but if we don't handle animal magnetism, it will claim to handle us. In my book, *Mindpower and the Spiritual Dimension*, I have gone to some lengths in exposing the "wiles of the serpent," but have gone on to show that Christian Science holds the remedy.

The claim of animal magnetism is that there is an opposite

to God. It claims to reverse the seven synonyms, and that just as God is divinely active good, evil is actively operative in the opposite direction. Evil is not passive; it is aggressive, and the general atmosphere of mortal thought is directly opposed to the advancing spiritual idea as expressed in Christian Science.

We are in the prophesied End Times when, as our Leader says, "evil increases and becomes the great red dragon, swollen with sin, inflamed with war against spirituality, and ripe for destruction. It is full of lust and hate, loathing the brightness of divine glory." (*Science and Health*) But also according to prophecy, the remedy for all error has unfolded in Christian Science. Revelation says the Dragon "deceiveth the whole world." The remedy is to remain undeceived by appearances. In its war against the advancing spiritual idea, the serpent is attacking our movement on several fronts — medical, theological, psychological and political. Also, the communications media today are far more pervasive and powerful than in Mrs. Eddy's time. In addition, mental and psychic systems are proliferating. Christian Science is still being attacked from the pulpits, while Roman Catholic priests consciously malpractice our movement. The Jesuits are trained in mental malpractice. Roman Catholics regard Christian Scientists as heretics. They pray for the death of heretics and work mentally to reverse the truths in *Science and Health.*

Even the Soviet Communists were malpracticing our movement. This is shown in the *Communist Manual of Psychopolitics* by Kenneth Goff, who turned from Communism when he realized what evil things they were up to. His testimony appears in Vol . 8 of the U. S. Congressional Report of 1939. The book includes these statements: "The psychopolitical operative should spare no expense in smashing out of existence, by whatever means, any actual healing group, such as acupuncture in China, Christian Science, dianetics and faith healing in the United States. The teachings of Mrs. Eddy must be swept aside. They must be discredited, defamed, arrested, stamped upon. . . .You must suborn district attorneys and judges into an intense belief. . . . that Christian Science or any other religious practice which might devote itself to mental healing is vicious, bad, insanity-causing, publicly hated and intolerable."

The methods to be used include hypnotism, telepathy, psychiatry, telekineses, brainwashing, and terror, which they say makes people pliant and obedient. One of their aims is to produce insanity in leaders, or get them classified as insane, so they can use drugs, or psychiatry, or brain surgery to alter their thinking or personality.

It is significant that Lenin, after reading *Science and Health* in Switzerland, said that Christian Science is the direct opposite of dialectical materialism, and he wrote something that is the reverse of the "scientific statement of being."

We need to realize that all materialistic thought constitutes mesmerism, but when it is actively promoted, becomes an aggressive mental force of which we need to be aware if we are to counter it. Nathan Talbot in an article in the French *Herald* of December 1983 on the subject of dialectical materialism said, "When developed and promoted as a truism by their believers, the belief becomes a malpractice, mental ill will, directed towards those who are praying for a purer discernment of God."

But nowhere have materialistic doctrines been able to alleviate human conditions in the way spiritual ascendancy and the Protestant ethic have done in the West. Churchill said, "There are two places where Marxist/Socialism will work — in Heaven, where it is not needed; and in Hell, where they already have it." Social and political doctrines based on materialism have no ultimate answers to human problems. The remedy for materialism is not more materialism, and if Christianity continues to dilute the spiritual gospel, the problems will go on being compounded.

It is those churches that have become spiritually bankrupt that become amenable to Marxism and resort to material means for alleviating distress. But since the world's aggravated problems are the result of materialism, merely changing material conditions leaves the basic problems unsolved. People can't go on dividing an ever-diminishing cake, and sooner or later mankind will have to turn to God, Spirit, as the source of limitless good.

Marxist materialism cannot supply mankind's need for a spiritual anchor. Because it has no fundamental basis for ethics, it cannot define the meaning and purpose of life. And if there is no life beyond the grave, and nobody questions what's beyond, existence is reduced to a wretched slavery to materialism.

Communism denies spirituality, devalues individuality, and fetters free will. It is a denial of spiritual reality, and therefore has no means by which to transcend itself, and man's spiritual roots wither in the drought of materialism. But because materialism has now become obsolete, even in the eyes of some physicists, all systems which are based on it are doomed. But the serpent is having its last fling.

An important aspect of this subject of animal magnetism is the degree to which we lay ourselves open to it by negative or sinful thinking. The shafts of error reach us through our undestroyed materiality, hence the importance of purifying and spiritualizing consciousness. There are two kinds of animal magnetism: the malicious and the delicious. When a preacher compiled a list of 457 sins, he was swamped with requests for the list by people who were afraid they were missing something.

One thing we must be clear on: animal magnetism is a lie, a false claim to power, but unless it is handled and reduced to nothing, it seems to affect people's lives and bodies and environment. Mrs. Eddy says, "The basic error is mortal mind." But there is no mortal mind, which is another name for nothingness. We must get back here to the absolute statement of Christian Science. The claim of animal magnetism is the claim of dualism, the belief that there is some mind, power, substance or reality other than one infinite God, Spirit, good. Rising above dualism to the monistic statement of Christian Science, we pray from the basis of divine Mind's absolute allness and omnipotence.

I would like to suggest an exercise for handling animal magnetism. Whenever you read in *Science and Health* or Mrs. Eddy's other writings about mortal mind or animal magnetism claiming to do something, this claim should be denied; and reversed by knowing the divine facts. For example, in "Ways that are Vain" in *Miscellany,* Mrs. Eddy says, "Animal Magnetism, in its ascendant steps of evil, entices its victim by unseen, silent arguments. Reversing the modes of good, in their silent allurements to health and holiness, it impels mortal mind into error of thought, and tempts into the committal of acts foreign to the natural inclinations," and so on. Well, here we have to be alert and deny that animal magnetism or mortal mind can do any such things. Unless we do this in our reading, we are liable to take it that this is what the serpent does, and unless we deny and reverse the claims there and then, we are liable to reinforce them as we read them.

The Healing Practice

Our Leader said that healing alone would save our movement and prosper it. Healing is proof of the authenticity of Christian Science, and it is significant that Jesus' proof of his Messiahship was to refer John to his healing works.

Because of the importance of healing to the prosperity of our Cause, it must be expected that the serpent's main endeavor would be to frustrate it — it seems with some measure of success. While we know that there is a lot of good healing work going on in the movement, it is plain that we need to do much better if our Leader's expectations regarding Christian Science are going to be fulfilled. She hoped that every Christian Church in America, and some in other lands, would understand Christian Science sufficiently to heal in Christ's name, and that "Christendom would be classified as Christian Scientists." (*Pulpit and Press*)

To achieve greater success, we need to spiritualize consciousness and handle animal magnetism in order to heal more effectively. Every healing in Christian Science involves obliterating some phase of animal magnetism. In handling the serpent, we need to be alert to its phases, wiles and disguises. It tries to hide itself as material conditions. By keeping our thought focused on matter, it would decoy us from uncovering and obliterating the culprit, mortal mind. All disease, disability, disaster, death, destruction, lack, are pictured delusions in mortal mind — ignorance of God. Once this is realized, it becomes easier to see through and reject error's spurious claims.

In addition to handling world beliefs, *materia medica,* and religious anathema, we may need in our practice to handle specific phases of animal magnetism pertaining to each claim, but never losing sight of the fact of the absolute allness of God, Spirit, and the consequent non-existence of any contrary power or belief. The claim of an opposite to God, Spirit, is dealt with through depriving it of any leg to stand on. It is *never* person, place, nor thing.

Every claim of animal magnetism is a claim of some opposite to God. We, therefore, deprive it of any such claims by reference to the seven synonyms for God. Since divine Principle is the only law and power governing the universe and man, there cannot be any lawless or nefarious power to act anywhere. Because the only Mind is God and is the Mind of everyone, there is no mortal mind or material intelligence to think or plan evil in any form. Life, being God's omni-activity, error has no life or activity by which to operate. Having no Truth to support it, error has no means of existing. In the infinitude of Love, there is no room for anything hateful or hurtful. Because of the allness of Spirit, there is no objective matter to provide a medium for error.

Every claim of error is some phase of mortal belief appearing at the door of thought, and must be handled there. It has no objective reality, no mind or intelligence or power, and therefore cannot do anything or cause anything. It cannot enter our thought if we are alert to reject its lies and correct them with the truth. If we realize that every claim coming to us is but a false picturing to be seen correctly, we lose belief in error and open the field of consciousness for Truth. The inverted images of animal magnetism are without power or activity, without intelligence or reality. In absolute Christian Science, of course, there is no such thing as animal magnetism, and it is important that we see it as nothing. But we have to *know* this and handle the belief, or it will claim to handle us.

We know that so-called material conditions are illusory pictures in mortal thought. Matter is the shadow cast by ignorance of spiritual reality. That's why it's pointless to shadow-box it, argue with it, or try to make it better, instead of dealing with the culprit, mortal mind, which is ignorance of God. Matter is solidified mortal thought, made up of false beliefs. It's like a hole in thought. This analogy was used by Daniel Cowan in his book, *Mind Underlies Spacetime.* Mr. Cowan, who identifies himself as a Christian Scientist, sets out to prove, through pure logic, that "All is infinite Mind and its infinite manifestation." He explains how matter *seems* to be but is not. It's because of a hole, or seeming absence of true knowledge, in our thinking. He uses as an analogy a pine board with a knot in it. If the knot is knocked out, there is a hole. But we are aware of the hole only because of the surrounding wood. Now, if we chip away all the wood around the hole, there is no longer any hole. It has no real identity except as a seeming absence of something.

Although the analogy isn't perfect, it does show how a seeming absence of something can appear to exist as a problem because of a hole in our thinking, a state of ignorance or false consciousness. Whatever appears to the material senses as a seeming absence of Spirit, Life, good, is a darkened area of consciousness, a hole in our thinking. Its remedy is not to do anything to the hole, but to enlighten consciousness with the truth of being. The

Christ is this light of Truth, the true or spiritual idea of everything, the truth that Jesus said would make us free. In Sci*ence and Health,* Mrs. Eddy writes, "Tumors, ulcers, tubercles, inflammation, pain, deformed joints, are waking dream-shadows, dark images of mortal thoughts, which flee before the light of Truth."

Through progressive spiritualization and dematerialization of thought, we grow into the understanding of God's absolute allness, and the nothingness of matter and evil. Right where error claims to be, there is only God appearing as the sole reality of existence. Nothing else exists but God and His perfect creation. Mrs. Eddy says, "The only intelligence or substance of a thought, a seed, or a flower, is God, the creator of it." (ibid)

Because of the absolute allness of God, all there is to a seed, flower, heart, stomach, head, leg, car, toaster, or computer, is the Mind that is both noumenon and phenomenon. Mrs. Eddy says, "Infinite-Mind creates and governs all, from the mental molecule to infinity." "Evil in all its forms is inverted good," as she also tells us in *Unity of Good.* In her expository statement on St. John's vision on Patmos (already quoted), she makes it clear "that what the human mind terms matter and spirit indicates states and stages of consciousness."

Leo Rosten, in his book, *The Story Behind the Painting,* says, "We see, not what is 'there,' but what we have been taught to see there — not what is 'real,' but what we have been conditioned to think of as real. . . . We see things as we are, not as they are." Professor Allen D. Allen of Wisconsin University says, "The capacity of the human senses for self-deception is nearly infinite."

All this surely shows that our primary need is to reflect the "Mind that was in Christ Jesus," as Paul adjures. Christian Science is the way. It reveals the allness of God, Spirit, good. Every problem is a seeming absence of God, a hole in our thinking, an inversion of reality. The remedy for every problem lies in the understanding of God. In Proverbs, we read, "With all thy getting, get understanding."

Matter, being the suppositional inversion of Spirit, good, we need to turn it right side up and see it correctly. That which enables us to turn it right side up is the Christ, Truth, defined by Mrs. Eddy as "the true idea, voicing good, the divine message from God to men, speaking to the human consciousness." Jesus wasn't taken in by these inversions when he "beheld in Science the perfect man, who appeared to him where sinning mortal man appears to mortals," and this true view "healed the sick," as Mrs. Eddy says.

Everything that comes to thought is a matter of conscious perception. The "out there" is the divine actuality *as it appears to spiritual perception.* It follows that the place where healing occurs is in our consciousness. As we prayerfully realize the absolute allness of Spirit, God, good, and understand the oneness of infinite Mind, universally reflected by man, this Christly consciousness heals by revealing the divine facts of being. The old method of addressing the human thought, of trying to change or heal something, is the dualistic sense that must be outgrown. Even if we say evil is a belief, this means someone is believing it, and we must unsee such a picture.

It's important to realize that Mrs. Eddy wrote the textbook to reach readers at various stages of understanding. It therefore contains relative as well as absolute statements which might appear conflicting unless this is understood. For example, she says sin and fear are causes of disease, and on page 419:10-12, she also says sin and fear have no power to cause disease. One is in the relative, the other in the absolute.

It is plain that Mrs. Eddy expected her followers to advance to the absolute standpoint which she says in *Miscellaneous Writings* is the way we must walk. Unless we understand this necessity we may get hung up with the relative or dualistic sense of Science, and make little progress. Mrs. Eddy makes clear in many passages her expectations that we should advance to the absolute standpoint.

The clearest statement is on page 242 of *Miscellany*. Here she writes: "Christian Science is absolute; it is neither behind the point of perfection nor advancing towards it; it is at this point and must be practiced therefrom." She then goes on to say, "Unless you fully perceive that you are the child of God, hence perfect, you have no Principle to demonstrate and no rule for its demonstration."

This is one of our Leader's most unequivocally monistic statements, implying that when you do understand that you are the child of God, hence perfect, you have the perfect Principle, and *every* rule for its demonstration. Man isn't a becoming, but a *divine being,* the very "expression of God's being."

Mrs. Eddy was concerned lest the Christian Science movement remain in the dualistic sense, operating from the basis of belief instead of on "a fixed eternal Principle, wholly apart from mortal conjecture," as she said in her important statement, "Principle and Practice," reprinted from the *Christian Science Sentinel* of Sept. 1, 1917. Here she makes the important distinction between faith healing and true spiritual healing in Christian Science on the basis of "fixed, eternal Principle." She warns of the loss of Christian Science healing unless it is understood and practiced therefrom.

It is, of course, true that many remarkable cures take place as a result of blind faith in God, and we can be grateful for them, but Mrs. Eddy's warning should be taken seriously, for it's quite apparent on analyzing many of the testimonies of healing in our movement that they occur on this secondary level.

Faith healing involves changes of belief, and beliefs are unpredictable and liable to change again. Faith healing works from the dualistic basis of a God "out there" who is asked to change something "down here" needing healing. The faith that asks God to heal implies that there is something "out of kilter" in His universe, that God isn't All, and that He needs to correct something. Faith cures are akin to the changes of belief that occur through hypnotism, voodoo, witchcraft, and psychic methods. These have no relationship to healing in Christian Science, and the same applies to the healings in other Christian churches, none of which have the monistic understanding of God's absolute allness which precludes the possibility of any matter or evil.

Faith cures occur when the strength of human belief causes it to see its own hopes or convictions objectified. The use of human will, the laying on of hands, the visualization of desired results, the use of formulas or mantras are all the paraphernalia of animal magnetism. Sure, we all need to have more faith, but it must be solidly based on the spiritual understanding of God's absolute allness and omnipotence.

It is often said that all religions worship the same God, but there's no doubt that their concepts of God are divergent, so it's doubtful that we all do worship the same God. Mrs. Eddy says, "The right understanding of God restores harmony." I, for one, don't worship an anthropomorphic God, or a God who causes natural disasters, sends disease, or allows a devil to wreak evil on His creation, or could be killed on a cross, or who sleeps, or who is afar off. Many people do believe in such a God, but that's the antithesis of the Christian Science God. We worship the living God who is Spirit, infinite Love, the source and condition of our very being. We don't think *about* God or Truth, but *as* Mind's very expression. It is Mind, God, Himself appearing as our Mind, the Mind that was also in Christ Jesus.

Christian Science is not a mere religion worshiping an unknown God. It is a demonstrable Science, "the divine Principle of all real being which [Jesus] taught and practised," as Mrs. Eddy said.

The vital distinction between the transcendent metaphysics of Christian Science and other transcendental systems is: *Science applies the supraphysical laws of Mind, the ever-*

operative divine Principle of the universe, to redeem the human condition, not to escape from it.

Because there is one all-inclusive infinity of Mind, the universe is not something external to our thinking. We see our concept of the universe reflected back to us. It will appear to us either according to our material beliefs, or according to our understanding of spiritual reality. The mortal view would hold the world in bondage to materialism, but the prayerful understanding of infinite spiritual perfection helps to thin out the mortal mist, and reveal more of the divine reality.

All experience is a function of consciousness, and it stands to reason that our habitual outlook will be reflected in our bodily experience. Mrs. Eddy refers to matter as an "alias" for mortal mind and the body as an "alias" for conscious thought. If the body is "conscious thought," then our habitual outlook on life can become manifested in negative bodily conditions. Jesus said, "The light of the body is the eye; if thine eye therefore be single [that is, monistic], thy whole body shall be full of light. But if thine eye be evil thy whole body shall be full of darkness."

I mentioned in my book, *Mindpower and the Spiritual Dimension,* the case of a woman whose body was full of darkness as a result of focusing on error. She was afflicted with five serious diseases, two of them being categorized as incurable. She wasn't a Christian Scientist, but having gone through a number of surgical operations, she had reached the stage where the best her family could hope for was that she would be released from her great suffering through death on the operating table. At this point, a Christian Science practitioner, whom I knew, was asked to take the case, and through her spiritual perceptivity she discerned that the woman's problem was but a manifestation of her extreme sensitivity to the sufferings and misfortunes of people in her community. Her sympathetic responses brought to her all the tragedies of the neighborhood, and her thought was filled with dark images which Mrs. Eddy 

equates with disease. Her tortured and pained thinking wasn't really able to help or heal any of their sufferings, but it was pictured in her body as the five diseases she had. This surely was a classic case of a "good person" suffering unjustly, but we need to realize that the subtlety of error often appears in the guise of human good.

The practitioner spoke to the woman of God's great love for all His children. She explained that there are two kinds of sympathy: one, in which we enter into the same pit with the sufferer to comfort him. This means there are now *two* in the pit. The other kind of sympathy is where the comforter remains outside the pit and lets down a rope to help the victim out. The practitioner showed that there is a rope that is able to rescue not only the victim but is able to help the others for whom she felt so deeply. The rope in this case being the tender, compassionate Spirit of Christ, the infinite love of God who "healeth all [our] diseases, who redeemeth [our] lives from destruction." This Christly Comforter reveals God's loving care for all His children, and it heals because it reveals what is really true about God and man as God's image and likeness. With the practitioner's prayerful help and the woman's own awakening spiritual sense, all the diseases were quickly healed.

This case also shows that doing good on a human plane doesn't really solve problems. In fact, it is often overlooked that human sympathy holds people in the claim of error and is a form of benevolent mesmerism. A misguided sense of caring and concern can innocently put upon others mental suggestions that may induce a claim of error.

The entire basis of evil inheres in false thought, the belief of life, substance and intelligence in matter and evil. *But there is no objective substance called matter.* It is only mortal mind's alias, called matter. Because everything is mental, there is no intractable or incurable problem. All problems are amenable to prayerful right thought. Our prayerful knowing of Truth is God disclosing Himself to us as our Mind and the Mind of everyone, including the so-called patient. This Christly light reveals to the patient his own Godlikeness, and this appears as healing.

Time has nothing to do with healing because all of Truth is true now. Spiritual illumination dispels the dark shadows or holes in thought with the truth of being. This illumination comes to us as the consciousness of Love's absolute allness. Fear, hate, inharmony of any kind, are unknown and unknowable in Love's realm. In this consciousness of Love's allness, we lose sight of both patient and practitioner, and that's when healings occur spontaneously.

Many of us have probably had such experiences when we've gotten ourselves out of the way. I can recall spontaneous healings of several so-called incurable diseases, including hereditary or congenital conditions. One was during a polio epidemic. I was in the office of the school where I worked when the phone rang. It was the Medical Officer at the Isolation Hospital, asking that a message be passed to the Health Inspector in the area to the effect that a woman had been admitted with polio, and requesting that the Health Officer visit her home in case further cases might appear. Even while the doctor was talking to me, I was vehemently denying — mentally, of course — that there was any such thing as a paralyzing fearful thought in the allness of divine Love to bind any of God's children. I said to myself, "I just don't believe in polio," but I passed the doctor's message on, as promised. The doctor phoned the next morning, and I wasn't surprised when he said the woman was well and had been released from hospital.

The fact that I had no feeling of personal responsibility in the case allowed free course for Truth. A sequel to this occurred not long afterwards when my wife, who was the school's secretary, received a phone call from the same doctor saying that a child had been admitted to the Isolation Hospital with paralytic polio and requesting the Health Inspector's assistance. My wife let the affluence of Truth and Love flood her consciousness as the doctor spoke. A day or two later the Health Inspector, in conversation with the doctor, was told that the child had been released, healed of the paralysis.

Mrs. Eddy said a grain of Truth can do wonders, and she told John Lathrop, "All I have ever accomplished has been done by getting Mary out of the way, and letting God be reflected. When I would reach this tone, the sick would be healed without a word." (*We Knew Mary Baker Eddy, First Series*) And she also told us that the way to instantaneous healing is through love. "Just live love — be it — love, love, love. Do not know anything but love. Be love. There is nothing else. That will do the work. It will heal everything; it will raise the dead. Be nothing but love."

The Comforter, the Final Revelation of Truth

Mrs. Eddy was the first since Christ Jesus to discern the absolute allness and omnipotence of God, Spirit, Mind, and the consequent non-existence of anything unlike Spirit, good. While Christ Jesus undoubtedly understood absolute Science, he could not reveal it to his immediate followers because they would not have understood him. Even some of his more radical statements caused his disciples to return to their fishing. Speaking of some of the deeper truths, he said, "Ye cannot bear them now," but he promised to send the Comforter to "teach [us] all things."

Christian Science is therefore a higher revelation. Mrs. Eddy realized she had to express its deeper meanings in such a way that they unfold to us only as we advance beyond the relative or dualistic sense of Science. This does not mean that we escape into a transcendentalism, but it does mean that we unsee the claims of error more readily, and improve our performance in healing.

In our practice of Christian Science, it is important to recognize that it is the Second Coming of the Christ, the Comforter promised in the Bible, "the Spirit of truth: whom the world cannot receive, because it seeth him not, neither knoweth him: but ye know him; for he dwelleth with you, and shall be in you." Here the personal pronouns he and him would be more correctly translated as it, for in the Greek every noun has gender, and in this case the "Spirit of truth" is given masculine gender, though obviously it does not refer to a person.

It is also important to recognize Mary Baker Eddy as the God-appointed and God-anointed revelator of this "Spirit of truth," which would teach us all things, as John records. Successful practice also demands a correct apprehension of man and Church. We see man and Church in relation to the unfolding idea expressed and operative in Christian Science. In proportion as we recognize, and rejoice in, this appearing of the divine idea in man, we will find people responding to this Christly view and being drawn to that where it is expressed.

Mrs. Eddy refers to the real man as Christ. This real man (and there is no counterfeit called a mortal) is already in Science and cannot be separated from it. He is the full and perfect expression of all the qualities of God. Now, when we see these qualities being expressed anywhere, we are in fact discerning some aspect of God and of true Church. We are also seeing something of man in God's image.

If on the other hand we think we see people, communities and situations as expressing the opposite of God's qualities, we are in fact denying His omnipresence and are actually malpractising. If we see our communities as comprising Catholics, Anglicans, Muslims, atheists, and so on, this also is malpractice and tends to hold them in such beliefs.

Nothing is going on anywhere but God expressing Himself, with man as His "full and perfect expression." We cannot legitimately hold to any contrary view, and if we are to redeem that view, it can only be done from the truly monistic standpoint of perfect God, perfect man, perfect everything — all spiritual. The world is our patient, and our Leader has given us the metaphysical tools for its redemption.

Nothing can hold back the dawn of Christian Science if we handle animal magnetism. The millennium is already here, and only a change of consciousness is required to reveal its universal presence. Our Leader says, "This Science of being obtains not alone hereafter in what men call paradise, but here and now; it is the great fact of being for time and eternity." In *Miscellaneous Writings* she says, "Life in and of Spirit" is "the sole reality of existence." In Hebrews Paul writes of faith as "the substance of things hoped for, the evidence of things not seen,"but the original Greek says, "Now faith is a mental realizing of things hoped for, a detection of things already fulfilled, not being seen by the bodily eye."

True Church

True church is us, insofar as we embody "the structure of Truth and Love, whatever rests upon and proceeds from divine Principle." Brick and mortar structures are only as useful as the spirituality of their congregations. In fact, Mrs. Eddy said, "Material organization has its value and peril . . . and is requisite only in the earliest period of Christian history." She said it "should be laid off," and, "continued organization retards spiritual growth." (*Retrospection and Introspection*) She was referring here to hierarchy, not to grass roots working together which she commended during the period after 1889, when she abolished centralization, until it was re-established in 1892. During that period, she said there was "a great revival of mutual love, prosperity, and spiritual power," and 112 new churches were formed.

Why, then, was hierarchy re-established? Only because her followers insisted on it, but against our Leader's sternest warnings. She told them, "If you organize again it will ruin the prosperity of our church. I have consented to whatever the church pleases to do, for I am not its keeper, and if she again sells her prosperity for a mess of pottage it is not my fault." (Letter to William Nixon, Clerk)

The problem with hierarchy is that when others are controlled and directed and have decisions made for them, it inhibits initiative, individual responsibility, and spiritual growth. People wait to be led or become apathetic and fear to innovate lest they step out of line. This is the "peril" Mrs. Eddy referred to and which has held back our movement from fulfilling her prediction, "if the lives of Christian Scientists attest their fidelity to Truth", . . . this century will see "Christendom classified as Christian Scientists." (*Pulpit and Press*)

At the time when hierarchy was re-established, there was no *Church Manual.* Mrs. Eddy used that experience, however, to include By-laws that would phase out hierarchy after she left us. She allowed it to continue while she was still with us, giving her time to revisions of the *Manual,* and establishing the Cause, while retaining her overall control. She designed the *Manual* in such a way that those clauses which allowed officials to control, direct, and make decisions for others, could become inoperable when she was no longer available to give her consent to them. There are twenty-nine consent clauses, and she refused to change any of them when implored to do so by the Directors because "they came from God," as she said. She also designed a Deed of Trust (*Manual p.* 128) to give a Board of four Directors charge over the Boston complex, but not over the Field. The Publishing Society's Deed of Trust gives the Trustees full power to manage its operations "upon their own authority."

None of this would stop any necessary functions from being adopted at local level, such as choosing lecturers, and those spiritually minded enough to teach. She left the textbooks, *Science and Health* and the Bible as our teachers and guides. Thus our inspired Leader freed us to look to God alone for guidance, inspiration, and sustenance. "Know, then, that you possess sovereign power to think and act rightly, and that nothing can dispossess you of this heritage and trespass on Love." (*Pulpit and Press)* This opens the way for untrammeled and limitless progress.

Authorized and Unauthorized Literature

Now I'd like to throw in some thoughts about "unauthorized literature." This is usually taken to mean any literature on Christian Science which is not specifically authorized or approved or published by Boston. There is much literature on Science today which is not put out by the Publishing Society. Some of it attacks Christian Science, and it might even be useful for class-taught students to know what the opponents of Science are saying so that work may be done about it. Unless we are aware of what the serpent is up to, we aren't likely to counter its lies. Some students of Science who aren't yet firmly grounded in their understanding might be affected by such literature, but I know of people who have come into Science as a direct result of such attacks which have made them investigate Science.

Likewise, I know of a number of people who have come into Christian Science through reading literature which borrows from Science and which many would regard as "unauthorized." That term does not appear in Mrs. Eddy's writings, and, in fact, she was much opposed to attempts to circumscribe what her followers should read. Once when the editor of the periodicals suggested that unauthorized literature should be gathered up and burned, Mrs. Eddy immediately sent in a repudiation and called it a "most wicked, proscriptive, unchristlike measure," "obnoxious" and "tyrannical."

The editor also had suggested that a committee be set up to decide what Scientists should read. To this Mrs. Eddy replied, "I consider my students capable, individually, of selecting their own reading matter and circulating it." She said that even those purporting to write on Christian Science "are uttering *some* truth," and thus should be left to "the breezes of God." The *Manual* Article VIII, Section 11, refers to literature which is "not correct in its statement of the divine Principle and rules and the demonstration of Christian Science," but it does not prohibit our reading it.

We need to keep abreast of the times and read widely. A good deal of exciting literature on scientific research is streaming out, and the demand is on Christian Science to lead and not trail behind. Even secular literature can stimulate us to think more deeply on Science.

Attempts to circumscribe our reading matter would be a form of thought control opposed to the unfolding spiritual idea. Our Leader said you "possess sovereign power to think and act rightly, and that nothing can dispossess you of this heritage and trespass on Love." (*Pulpit and Press*)

Truth is its own power and protection. The poet Milton said: "And though all winds of doctrine were let loose to play upon the earth, so let Truth be in the field. We do injuriously by licensing and prohibiting to disdoubt her strength. Let Truth and Falsehood grapple; and who ever knew Truth put to the worse in a free and open encounter?" (Areopagitica)

The fact that the copyright on *Science and Health* has been overturned has not resulted in a distorted version appearing, but even if it did, the essential truth would prevail. In *Science and Health* Mrs. Eddy writes, "This book may be distorted by shallow criticism or malicious students, and its ideas may be temporarily abused and misrepresented; but the Science and truth therein will forever remain to be discovered and demonstrated." Just think how the Bible has been mistranslated, yet its essential message remains in all the different renderings.

Myriads of Bibles in numerous languages have gone out into the world, and each translation is colored with the translator's interpretation, yet it continues to leaven the world's thought. People are studying the Bible as never before, and wonderful demonstrations are being reported around the world.

Preeminently, Christian Science is the Science of divine Love. It is warmly Christian, not coldly scientific. Unutterably kind, compassionate, and unselfish in its ministrations, it demonstrates the Christly love our Master practiced. It unsees the mortal scene as an inverted view of reality.

From the vantage point of true monism, we can see everyone and all the activities in the world as, in fact, the expression of God and His Christ, no matter how seemingly material or evil they may appear to the material senses.

Christian Science with its divine metaphysics is in the vanguard of the conceptual revolution which is sweeping the world. There are great stirrings in human thought, and this is also being reflected in the churches. Dogmas are being revised, and the Holy Spirit is revitalizing Christianity. It is also being reflected in the numerous mental systems, philosophies and cults that are propagating more mental views of things. The activity of the Christ-idea in human consciousness is mentalizing matter as a prelude to "the final spiritualization off all things" that Mrs. Eddy foresaw. (*Miscellany*) The Great Red Dragon's magnified pictures of wars, hatred, violence, crime, famine, pollution, inflation, unemployment and economic turmoil show that material beliefs are being broken up under the impact of Christian Science.

The natural sciences have reached a watershed, and their material foundations are dissolving beneath them. Dr. Edmund Sinnott, Dean of Yale's Sheffield Scientific School, said there is need for some substantial anchor amid the collapse of old physical theories. He said that because matter in the old sense has ceased to be, the way is opening up for more idealistic and spiritual views of the universe. Their only possible direction now is transcendence into the spiritual perception of reality.

Supply

Christian Science, as the final revelation of Truth, has the ultimate answers to all the problems and limitations incidental to a material sense of existence. Some people object that there can be no "final" revelation, and this is true if that revelation is static and circumscribed, but Christian Science reveals the ever-unfolding infinitude of Mind. The belief that life, substance and intelligence are material is fundamental to all human problems whether of health, supply, relationships, economy, or politics.

The world has now come to the stage where the imperative demand is upon Christian Scientists to demonstrate this Science of divine reality and its limitless potential. Mankind is being driven to look beyond matter to the spiritual source and resources of being.

We have already seen that a material basis is obsolete, and by realizing that everything is mental, the solution to the problem of supply, whether of health or wealth, is brought a step nearer.

The spiritual ideas which constitute substance are infinite, and "man reflects infinity," as Mrs. Eddy says. We need to think constantly in terms of the infinitude of good. The substance of spiritual ideas is as limitless as spiritually right thought. Ideas cannot be limited, cornered, divided, inflated, deflated, or cut off. The superabundant ideas ever pouring forth from infinite Mind are our substance and supply, equal to every human need. Mrs. Eddy's statement about Love meeting human needs demands of us the expression of that love in our daily lives. We live at the standpoint of limitless expression, and of limitless opportunity, and of divine fulfillment and completeness.

It is significant that the word *substance* comes from the same Latin root as the word *understanding* (*substare; sub* meaning under, and *stare* that which supports or stands under). Mrs. Eddy uses the word *substance* in relation to Mind, to Soul, Spirit, Life, Truth, Love, and to intelligence. She says those who believe substance to be matter are opponents of Christian Science. Perhaps we should examine ourselves to see to what degree we are opponents of Christian Science.

In the divine economy, supply and demand are coordinate ideas of Mind, and it is Love's purpose to hold them in perfect balance in order to bless both giver and receiver. There is always a supply for demand, and a demand for supply. For every legitimate need, the supply already exists. No idea ever lacks that which is necessary to express its completeness. A want is not necessarily a need, and Jesus said our requests for supply to indulge ourselves are not likely to be met. This is illustrated in a story of a little girl who prayed for a new bicycle. Her brother was skeptical of prayer, and when the little girl's prayers went unanswered, he said, "You see, God doesn't answer prayer." She replied, "Oh, yes He does. He said, No!"

Wanting something is a denial that we have it, and Jesus said, "What things soever ye desire, when ye pray, believe that ye receive them, and ye shall have them." Science operates from the basis that man is already complete and perfect, having all the good that the Father expresses. Because good is entirely spiritual, we have it in proportion to our spiritualized consciousness and our expression of God's qualities.

When Jesus told Peter to cast a line and find the tax-money in the mouth of the first fish he caught, he was showing that thought should be open to the infinite possibilities by which supply may come. We should never outline because that implies a separation and limitation. Supply is present everywhere because God, good, is everywhere.

It was Jesus' spiritual understanding of this divine fact that enabled him to manifest whatever was humanly needed anywhere, anytime. The Christ, the true idea of everything, comes to us where we are, at our present level of understanding, meeting our needs, and showing God's love for His children. But this coming of the Christ to the flesh is really meant to lead us to higher and higher understanding until the absolute is reached.

Everything in human experience symbolizes some spiritual idea, but the symbol and the idea are not two different entities. They are only different *views* of the one reality. Spiritual understanding translates ideas into sustenance for the human need, as Jesus showed with the loaves and fishes. But in Christian Science, we do not simply aim at having our human needs met. We aim at the ultimate understanding whereby we will be clothed and fed *spiritually,* as Mrs. Eddy foreshadowed in *Science and Health.* She said, "Christ, Truth, gives us temporary food and clothing until the material, transformed with the ideal, disappears, and man is clothed and fed spiritually."

In one story in the New Testament; we see three conceptual levels regarding supply illustrated. The lowest, or human level, was when the disciples went back to their fishing, after Jesus' crucifixion. Despite all their Master had taught them, their thought was still anchored to matter as substance, and after fishing all night, they had caught nothing. Jesus appeared on the shore and told them to cast the net "on the right side," to "launch out into the deep," and now "they were not able to draw it, for the multitude of fishes." It is not to be implied, as one commentator surmised, that Jesus, from his vantage point on the shore, could see where the fish were. Casting the net on the right side, or launching into the deep, imports the need to look to the deeper spiritual realities instead of matter.

Jesus' understanding enabled him to see real substance or supply as ever available ideas of infinite Mind. Fish are ideas in universal Mind, and because ideas are infinite, this Christly understanding translates into temporal food to meet needs at humanity's particular stage of understanding. Mrs. Eddy says, "Christian Science translates Mind, God, to mortals." (*Miscellaneous Writings*) Jesus translated spiritual ideas into what the disciples saw as fishes in their nets, and loaves and fishes for the multitude.

The disciples found that Jesus on the shore already had "a fire of coals there, and fish laid thereon, and bread." He did not need to go through the processes of catching fish or making bread. His spiritual understanding enabled him to translate spiritual ideas directly into the human perception of fish and bread.

need & supply are one!

Plainly, Jesus was showing the disciples — and us — the limitless possibilities of spiritualized consciousness. In an early issue of *The Christian Science Journal* (Vol.IV, p.94), Mrs. Eddy is recorded as saying, after a party, that she expected her followers one day to be able to enjoy the delectables without going through the conventional processes. But she obviously also saw beyond that to the ultimate state of understanding where "man is clothed and fed spiritually."

This understanding is relevant in our work on community, national and international problems of supply, such as famine, inflation, unemployment, and other beliefs of limitation associated with materialism. God's business of being All-in-all includes no limitation in any direction, and man, as His "full and perfect expression," includes all that God is expressing.

All business is God's business and expresses limitless abundance. Its purpose is to bless. There are no fluctuations or cycles in the infinitude of good. Beliefs of stagnation or lack or loss cannot touch true business because business is the activity of Mind, God. Loss, lack and stagnation are mortal beliefs not actual conditions. Business is in us, and we bring to bear on it the qualities of our own thinking. Business can't think; it doesn't know whether it is good or bad, and we have dominion in proportion to our spiritual understanding of substance, supply, and true business.

Many people have demonstrated dramatic turn around from failing businesses to successful ones through spiritually understanding these realities. Mind has infinite ways of employing man in expressing the qualities of God.

What do we do about the headlines nowadays, about millions of people perishing from starvation, homelessness, unemployment, overpopulation? During the next twenty years, the world's population will be doubled. This means that all the development that has taken place in the world up till now will need to be doubled, including all the facilities for living. Mexico City now has 18 million inhabitants and is so polluted that merely breathing its air is equivalent to smoking 40 cigarettes a day. The city produces 6000 tons of rubbish a day more than it can collect. Similar problems are cropping up in various parts of the world.

Mass famine, and the crime it generates, loom ahead. How do Christian Scientists respond to all this? Like every other problem, it boils down to the claim of animal magnetism that everything is material, and man a creator. Everything about matter is limitation, but Christian Science and even the physicists tell us that matter isn't substantial, that it's an illusion, and that everything is mental. Christian Science has come to show that everything is spiritually mental, the creation of God, Mind, who is infinite and entirely good.

This puts a completely new complexion on the world situation. Healing in Christian Science comes through understanding the realities of being right where the material unreality seems to be. There are not two realities — one material and imperfect and another spiritual and perfect. The world and everything in it is not a creation to be made perfect, any more than a diseased body has to be changed.

Mrs. Eddy says, "There is but one creator, and one creation." She also tells us that to the unillumined human mind it appears material, while to spiritualized consciousness it appears spiritual. She says, "Mortal existence is a dream" — an illusion. All that appears out there as a surging world of hungry, warring, sinful, constricted mortals, and a polluted earth is the unillumined human mind's pictured delusion about the spiritual creation which is the only reality. Mrs. Eddy says, "For right reasoning there should be but one fact before the thought, namely, spiritual existence." The kingdom of heaven in which we live, move and have our being, is the present reality. Man reflects the infinity of Mind, Soul, and its perfect ideas. God's immortal children reflect every good quality and condition. Inasmuch as matter, space and time are obsolete human concepts, there can be no pressure of space for living, no depletion of the limitless resources of Soul. In the pure atmosphere of Spirit, pollution is impossible. In the realm of infinite Love, man lives eternally as the blessed child of God, rejoicing in the harmony, peace and superabundance of good that God is forever expressing. God is ever employing man in expressing His qualities, and He rewards man for so doing. This isn't a dream picture, but the reality; and in proportion as we unequivocally hold to it and reject the lie, we will help the world to see it.

Mankind's greatest need is not for material wealth, food, clothing, houses, jobs or healthy matter. It is for the spiritual understanding which translates the limitless ideas of Mind into humanly perceptible supply. The situation in the world today appears one in which increasing demands are being made for us to help the poor and needy. The question frequently arises whether Christian Science churches should contribute to charities, and individual members often wonder which to support, whether to support, or how much to contribute. Individuals make their own decisions in these matters, but as far as branch churches are concerned, perhaps they should follow the Mother Church's example. It confines its giving to cases of national and international emergencies. Otherwise it is likely that with the pressing demands of humanity today, we might dissipate resources that should go to promoting the Science which meets all human needs in the right way. Because of the compassion we feel, it is hard to resist supporting reputable charities, but our purpose is to heal lack at its source and not become deflected into human means and methods.

Many of the other church denominations are heavily engaged in human ways of doing good, through social work, famine relief, hospital care, and other means. We can be grateful for such Christian endeavors, but that isn't the Christian Science way of healing the problems. Those means often compound the problems by reinforcing materialistic beliefs, dulling initiative and encouraging dependence. They don't heal the problems. Christian Science shows the way to heal and how to dispense with charity.

Mrs. Eddy quotes a Talmudical philosopher on this subject: "The noblest charity and the best alms are to show and enable a man to dispense with alms." Our first priority then should be to strengthen and support the promotion and extension of Christian Science by which mankind can overcome the beliefs of lack. Christian Science alone has the remedy.

You have probably heard of the book, *God's Smuggler,* by Brother Andrew, who has smuggled millions of Bibles into countries where they are restricted. He now heads a worldwide organization for distributing the Scriptures. To support this work, dinners are held in various centers where couriers tell of their own experiences. In 1981 a million Bibles were carried to China in a barge, and Christians there say they need millions more.

At one of these dinners held in Boston recently, a courier told of his experience in taking Bibles into Mocambicque, a Marxist country in Africa, where the Scriptures are restricted. The courier was from the adjoining country of Malawi. In response to his own prayers he was led to put five hundred Bibles into his white car and head for the border. A border official asked if he had any Bibles, and it came to him to say, facetiously, "Yes, my car is full of Bibles." He was rebuked for his jocularity and told to get on his way.

The courier still had no idea where to deliver the Bibles, but through prayer, he was led to go to a certain city. Only later did he learn that a pastor had set out with an assistant on a two day walk to that city, having seen in a vision a white car bringing much needed Bibles. He saw a white car standing at a gas station and recognized it from his vision. Walking up to the car, he knocked on the window and said, "I think you have something for me — Bibles." One can imagine the tears of joy at that meeting. It is reminiscent of some of the stories in the Scriptures.

The Spirit of Christ is active in human consciousness and nothing can block it. There can be little doubt that the great ground swell in religious renewal seen in the Western world today is due to the unfolding spiritual idea promoted by Christian Science and more than one thousand church denominations now practice healing. The word is going forth through our literature, lectures, prayers, and church services. It cannot return void, and we should place no limitations on it.

Someone, somewhere, must have prayed in support of the evangelizing mission of our periodicals when a man, in the depths of despair, found a *Christian Science Sentinel* in a dustbin. It changed his life. I recall a story many years ago about a woman who had reached the end of her tether and decided to commit suicide. It was a cold, wintry night, and she went to a bridge intending to jump into the river below. While contemplating this desperate step, she felt a piece of paper blow against her leg. She picked it off, and on it she read something relating to Christian Science. She decided to follow it up, and it changed her life. There must have been prayer somewhere behind that event.

Healing The World

Most of us seem too preoccupied with personal and parochial problems to expand our prayerful work to heal the world. Yet this is what Mrs. Eddy expected of us as she makes clear in the opening pages of the *Manual* where she says the Church is for "healing and saving the world." This surely must include the "greater works" that Christ Jesus expected of his followers.

We cannot place limits on the power of the Christ to redeem the world. No problem is too big for the Christly understanding of the absolute allness and omnipotence of God, Spirit, good. Truth is omnipotent and is operative everywhere. It operates by illuminating consciousness with the light of Christ, not by eliminating evil as an entity or power. There is no opposite to God, the All-in-all. Prayer that hopes God will act on something "out there" is dualistic and is the traditional Christian way that hasn't redeemed the world in two thousand years.

Problems, of whatever magnitude, are nothing more than false thought objectified, and false thought is correctable through the prayerful understanding of Mind's omnipotence and omnipresence. Corruption, immorality, crime, racism, terrorism, wars, and so on, are no more substantial than false thought. The matter through which they appear to be manifested is likewise an entirely mental phenomenon. No matter how big or threatening, evil is not a thing, but a false picture in mortal mind. It isn't going on since "God is everywhere, and nothing apart from Him is present or has power," as Mrs. Eddy states in the textbook.

Ideas have power. No, spiritual ideas *are* power because they are divine Mind's very expression, whereas false concepts of mortal thought have no power, no intelligence, no substance, no medium, no activity, except insofar as they are believed. But false beliefs cannot sustain themselves when the Christly light of God's allness outshines them.

Governments and institutions are only systems of thought. This makes them amenable to spiritually-right thought. I know this is demonstrable as our last trip to America showed. We had been giving thought to this trip, and when the time seemed right, we began to make definite plans. The first hurdle was to obtain an increased travel allowance. Due to the war situation in Rhodesia, the allowance was very small, and the country was extremely short of foreign exchange. The bank said there was little chance of it being granted, but I knew that a right idea includes all that is necessary for its fulfillment, and we wished to attend the Annual Meeting in Boston where I had been invited to a meeting for contributors to the periodicals. The extra allowance was granted.

We then proceeded with drawing up the complicated itinerary, having had invitations to stay with friends in various States, and we also wished to visit a number of beauty spots. When we applied for visas, the American Consulate in Johannesburg issued these after satisfying themselves that I was no longer working for what they called the "rebel Rhodesian Government." Later, however, my wife noticed that a double-entry visa would be necessary as we intended visiting Canada, then returning for the Annual Meeting in Boston.

On phoning the Consulate, I explained the situation but was told they had had instructions from Washington that no Rhodesians were to be allowed double-entry visas. I explained that the itinerary had been finalized and all the bookings made. Still the response was negative, but I just *knew* it would be overturned because a Bible verse had stood out to me as though illumined. It was from I Chronicles 16, and said: "When they went from nation to nation, and from one kingdom to another people, He suffered no man to do them wrong: Yea, He reproved kings for their sakes."

How could one doubt with such a promise? The Consul must have felt the activity of the spiritual idea, and since I persisted, he said, "Well, send us your passports and we'll see what we can do." We received them back, not merely with double-entry visas, but triple-entry visas! Then, a few days before we were due to leave, we discovered we'd need visas for Brazil since we intended spending a few days there on the way to New York. The travel agent assumed we knew about this, so hadn't told us. I said I'd fly to Johannesburg to get the visas, but he said, "That's no good, because the Consul lives a thousand miles to the south in Cape Town, and all applications have to be sent to Brazil, and it never takes less than a month."

Still, I had no feelings of concern. I just knew it would work out because that morning another Bible verse had stood out for me. It was from Revelation, and read: "Behold, I have set before thee an open door, and no man can shut it." I asked the travel agent to telex the airlines representative in Rio de Janiero to tell him we were coming.

When we were finalizing the usual formalities preparatory to boarding the plane, we were suddenly told we couldn't go because we had no visas for Brazil. They said the airline would be heavily fined, and we would be put in jail on arrival.

But mortal mind was foxed because I had taken the precaution of booking straight through to New York, and we were then allowed to embark. On arrival at Rio airport, we were met on the airport and asked if we were Mr. and Mrs. Haw. We were then instructed to follow the official but warned to say nothing to anybody. He disappeared for about twenty minutes and then came out and mounted a dais.

He beckoned us forward, then gave us slips of paper authorizing us to enter Brazil while our passports were held.

This shows that we don't have to accept limitations or restrictions on a right purpose, even if the regulations might say otherwise.

Because institutions and regulations are systems of thought, spiritually right thought can change them. Our whole trip, covering some 50,000 kilometers, was a marvelous demonstration throughout, even over weather conditions which on two occasions appeared to be miraculously changed.

Inasmuch as the whole of mortal existence is an inversion of spiritual reality, we need to see it all correctly and know the truth that reverses it. From the standpoint of absolute Science, all space is filled with God, good, and evil doesn't exist; but we need to do our prayerful work about it since evil seems a frustrating or menacing claim if unhandled.

From time to time we hear of cases where Science has healed community problems involving crime, corruption, strikes and riots. I had an experience not long ago which showed how prayer can have a community-wide impact. The local newspaper one day carried a report of a particularly despicable and violent attack on a defenseless and innocent woman. My initial reaction to the report was one of outrage, but I quickly realized this was the serpent's attempt to get me to think that evil is real and powerful. I immediately turned from this tack and got on my metaphysical high horse. And, from the vantage point of God's allness and omnipotence, I vehemently declared the counterfacts, knowing they carried the authority of divine law. The "I," of course, is Mind, God, Truth knowing itself.

We sometimes need to be vehement in our declarations as our Leader points out on pages 420 and 421 of *Science and Health*. There was a story in a Christian Science lecture many years ago about a farmer whose kitchen door had two of those little openings at the bottom for the cats to go in and out. When he was asked why he needed two openings, he said, "Well, I have two cats, and when I say 'scat,' I mean scat!" A vehement rejection of error's claims often demolishes their mental support.

Working on that newspaper report, I told the serpent to scat with its mesmeric lies about crime and immorality. I denounced mortal mind as the criminal and deprived it of any law, power, intelligence, personality, or any arena in which to operate. I declared man's innocency and purity, including, of course, the so-called criminal.

I saw man — all men — as reflecting and embodying the qualities of God as defined by the seven synonyms. I saw divine Principle as operating everywhere and maintaining perfect order and control.

I saw divine Love as supplying all human needs, and therefore there could be no necessity for theft or robbery or violence since everyone is complete, satisfied, and abundantly provided for.

I let my prayer flood over the whole community, embracing all in the one divinity, including so-called criminals. In the Bible, we read, "When thou sawest a thief, thou consentest with him." This I took to mean that a thief is a mental image in mortal mind, a false concept of man, and the healing must therefore take place in consciousness. Man reflects the integrity and honesty of Principle and is not a criminal. Mortal mind's lies have nothing to do with person, place or thing — though it may appear as such. Error cannot resist or escape the truth that exposes its nothingness.

I gained a sense of Love's allness and dominion and was at peace, then I went on with my reading. Listening to the radio the next morning, I was awed to hear the police chief's report that something unique had happened that night. Not a single crime against person or property had been reported in the entire region, with its nearly three million inhabitants.

I realized, of course, that this result had nothing to do with Richard Haw, but was the action of the Christ-power representing the Ruler of the universe. We all can do more in following Mrs. Eddy's injunction to "hold crime in check," and "maintain law and order" by utilizing the limitless power and potential of God's law as expressed and operative in Christian Science.

Community, national and international problems, though seemingly large and formidable, are not more real than small problems. They are not anything more substantial than universal false belief. 2000 + 2000 =5000, is not more formidable than 2 + 2 = 5, and no matter how many zeroes are strung out, it doesn't make it more real. No matter how large a problem seems to be, God remains All, omnipotent. No problem is too great for the divine Mind which we reflect. In fact, there are no real problems — only opportunities to prove the allness and omnipotence of God.

We are all familiar with Mrs. Eddy's statement in *Science and Health* where she says, "One infinite God, good, unifies men and nations, constitutes the brotherhood of man, ends wars," and so on. As it is generally read, most of us would be inclined to think of God correcting these errors, but this would be dualistic. Some of you may know my friend, Dorothy Rieke, who puts this passage into the monistic or absolute standpoint in this way: "Because of one infinite God, good, men and nations are unified, — all men love each other, and are aware of being brothers. There are no wars, no hates, no conflicts. There is no pagan or Christian idolatry. All of

God's children are equal, and everything is right in social, civil, criminal, political and religious codes. All men are blessed by the one infinite divine Mind. And not only is there nothing that can sin, suffer, be punished or destroyed, but everything is harmonious. All men are holy, healthy, comfortable, being preserved by their heavenly Father, and rewarded by Him. That's the way it is, because of the allness of the one infinite God, good."

Christian Science is the law of God, omnipotent and omnipresent Principle, and because there is no other power or presence, there is nothing to oppose or withstand Truth's knowing of its own infinitude. Because there is but one infinite God, omnipotent and omni-active Mind, there is no mortal mind to project delusions of evil, sin, disease, death or disaster. But we have to know this, understand it, and claim it. Though the way to handle animal magnetism in Christian Science is simple, when we understand the unequivocal allness of divine Mind, God, the work calls for our dedication and alertness.

The unfolding spiritual idea demands that we advance in our understanding. Yesterday's understanding isn't always adequate for today's challenges. Unless we are advancing, we are like a canoeist on a river being carried downstream by the current, and the water usually becomes more polluted the further we go downstream. There's no standing still; either we row upstream, or the currents of error will draw us downward.

Challenges are really opportunities to demonstrate what we know. We often yearn for surcease, but being comfortable in error shows we aren't growing in our understanding. Mrs. Eddy was suspicious of those who had no problems for she said if we are advancing spiritually, we would have plenty to meet. It stands to reason that the more we understand of Truth the more its suppositional opposite will come up to be destroyed. The serpent won't bother us if we are on his side.

Not that our lives should be constantly stormy, but in advancing spiritually, we are challenging entrenched materialism which resists its destroyer, Truth. Challenges and problems exercise our spiritual fibre and give us opportunities to demonstrate what we are learning in Christian Science. Isaiah says, "When the enemy shall come in like a flood, the spirit of the Lord shall lift up a standard for the people." A standard represents an emblem of Deity, a symbol of wisdom and power. Our standard is emblematic of God's omnipotence and omnipresence:

Equipped with the spiritual understanding of God's absolute allness, we can be sure that problems, which are really unillumined states of thought, cannot withstand the light and power of Christ, Truth. It was Jesus' understanding of God's allness, omnipotence and perfection and his oneness with God that enabled him to perform his works. And it can do the same for us in the degree that consciousness is spiritualized and our lives are imbued with Christly love, which our Leader tells us is "the vital part, the heart and soul of Christian Science."

Do we really love with that impartial and universal sense of love that simply loves regardless? It isn't easy, as we all know, but the world needs it. In the *Sentinel* of July 13, 1966, a healing of hate is treated which shows the potential of Christian Science for healing such problems. It involved two farmers. One was a big landowner, and the other was one of the neighboring tenants who were continually stealing and damaging his crops and property. Resentment finally built up to the point where the landowner became so furious after an incident that he got on his horse, determined to punish his neighbor. But as he rode along, a strange feeling came over him, an overwhelming feeling that dissolved all hatred. He felt an all-encompassing peace and dismounted his horse to sit under a tree, trying to figure out this change. Presently he saw two men coming down the road towards him. One was the neighbor and the other was the village mayor who was a friend of both of them.

The mayor asked if these quarrels couldn't be settled, and the landowner straightaway replied: "Yes, Mayor, from now on this man and I are going to be friends." They shook hands, and there were no further quarrels or incidents. But the climax didn't come till some time later. The landowner had a yearning to find an explanation to his change of heart. About a year later while visiting New York, he came across *Science and Health* and learned a little about Science. When he returned home to Cuba, he decided to attend the Christian Science services, and he was astonished to see his neighbor there. Afterwards they got to talking, and the neighbor explained what had happened that afternoon. He said his wife was a Christian Science practitioner, and that time when they met on the road, she was praying about the situation.

What a tremendous opportunity we have for healing the divisiveness and alienation in the world. Because there is but one infinite Mind, Love, one divine consciousness, this truth is a law of harmony and unity to any discordant situation. In the allness of Mind, there is no room for mortal opinions to hold sway. In the divine understanding, there can be no misunderstandings.

How are we seeing our neighbors, our politicians, our world? Fundamentally, our view simply reflects our understanding of God. Negative views reflect a deficient understanding of God. Our primary need, therefore, is to gain a deeper spiritual understanding, and this will outshine the error. The acid test of our understanding of God as Love would be to put ourselves in the shoes of the Good Samaritan in Jesus' parable and ask ourselves how we would conduct ourselves if the victim of the robbers happened to be our worst enemy?

The world situation may appear frightening to mortal sense, but we should recognize this as the result of Truth stirring and exposing error preparatory to its destruction. Viewed thus, the world scene should appear encouraging to Christian Scientists! We can see the prophecy Mrs. Eddy made on pages 96 and 97 of *Science and Health* being fulfilled. She told us, "The breaking up of material beliefs" would be seen as "famine and pestilence, want and woe, sin, sickness and death, which assume new phases until their nothingness appears." So what we are witnessing is "the breaking up of material beliefs," and Mrs. Eddy added, "This material world is even now becoming the arena for conflicting forces. On one side there will be discord and dismay; on the other side there will be Science and peace."

Dorothy Rieke renders the passage like this from the monistic standpoint: "There is no material world. Thus there is no arena for conflicting forces. Since the only world is that of God's creating, it is spiritual, harmonious, perfect. There is only one force — the force of the infinite supreme Being, which is a force for good. In this spiritual world there cannot be two sides — there's only one side, that of Science and peace. This truth annihilates, eliminates, exterminates, obviates even the possibility of a side that would be discordant, or would cause dismay. Oh, how wonderful it is that there are no material beliefs to breakup. All is infinite Mind and its infinite manifestation.

"Thus, the universe is filled with divine concepts. Because there is no mortal mind, there can be no material beliefs. Thus, there can be no manifestation of such things as famine and pestilence, want and woe, sin, sickness and death. Instead, there is but the manifestation of plenty, of perfection, supreme joy, righteousness, a scientific sense of health, and life eternal.

"A disturbance that never existed cannot continue. Never having occurred, it cannot recur. 'To Truth there is no error, all is Truth,' Mrs. Eddy tells us. Truth has ever been All-in-all. That is enough to guarantee that the universe is truly the manifestation of that which is harmonious and infinitely good."

The only place where evil may seem to exist is at the door of thought, and it is handled there as animal magnetism. A few years ago, I had occasion to put this into practice while traveling in terrorist-ridden country. (That's what mortal mind called it.)

At the height of the bush war in Rhodesia, I visited that country and traveled some 2000 kilometers by car through areas riddled with so-called terrorists. It was obvious, however, that prayerful work was called for, because of the strong human belief in danger. But I had no fear. I realized that true safety had nothing to do with being in a particular material environment. True safety is in divine consciousness, "the secret place of the most High," in which *everyone* dwells. The divine omnipresence could include nothing unlike good — no evil, violence, war, hatred, death or destruction; only, all-encompassing Love and its qualities of harmony, unity, peaceableness, joy, freedom and brotherhood.

My prayers embraced all in the one divinity in the realm of God where divine Principle, Love, reigns supreme. I felt perfectly safe because I understood there is no outside to God's infinite and perfect realm. Our entire visit was happy and harmonious.

The allness of God precludes the possibility of anything unlike good, and the prayerful understanding of His omnipresence and omnipotence cannot be limited or confined by any mortal beliefs to the contrary. We must rise to the absolute standpoint of Science in which all errors of belief are exposed as nothingness. The moral chemicalization we are witnessing is only the carnal mind's resistance to the unfolding spiritual idea, but it is yielding. Truth is at work in human consciousness, silently dislodging and dissolving erroneous beliefs.

All-inclusive divine consciousness, which we reflect, knows nothing but its own infinite expression. Mrs. Eddy says, "The divine understanding reigns, is all, and there is no other consciousness." That is our only true consciousness. The Truth we know and declare is Mind's own disclosure of its presence and therefore carries all the power and authority of the divine Principle of the universe. The Ninety-first Psalm says, "He that dwelleth in the secret place of the most High shall abide under the shadow of the Almighty." This is not a haven where we are hidden while evil rages without. It is a divine state of consciousness in which evil is

an impossibility because of the allness of God. There is no other reality but the realm of one infinite God, good. Into this infinitude of divine consciousness "can enter nothing that defileth or maketh a lie." Our mental work involves including everyone and everything in this citadel of conscious harmony and perfection.

The term *protective work*, however, implies there's something out there from which we need protection. We may then be inclined to place ourselves in a sort of mental fort to defend ourselves from evil outside.

Mrs. Eddy tells us that evil is destroyed, not by *declaring* there is none, but by *knowing* there is none. We have been given the exterminator of error and should use it. Our Leader says, "Mind is God. The exterminator of error is the great truth that God, good, is the *only* Mind." And because Christian Science is not a mere transcendentalism that doesn't deal with error, she goes on to give it specific denial, saying, "that the supposititious opposite of infinite Mind — called devil or evil — is not Mind, is not Truth, but error, without intelligence or reality."

We need to do this exterminating work on whatever claims of error present themselves in our daily lives, in our homes, at our offices, on the streets, when reading newspapers, or watching television. We cannot isolate ourselves in ivory towers, ignoring the claims of error, temporizing with it, or brushing it under the carpet.

Anything that comes to our consciousness becomes our responsibility, and if we don't do what our Leader expected of us, who else will? or can?

Mrs. Eddy declared, "What remains to lead on the centuries . . . is man in the image and likeness of the Father-Mother God." We all have that sacred charge that Christ Jesus gave us to fulfill, to "go the lost sheep of the house of Israel. And as ye go, preach, saying, The kingdom of heaven is at hand: Heal the sick, cleanse the lepers, raise the dead; cast out devils: freely ye have received, freely give."

For further information regarding Christian Science:

Write The Bookmark
Post Office Box 801143
Santa Clarita, CA 91380

Call 1-800-220-7767

Visit our website: www. thebookmark.com